Richard Lederer's

Ultimate Book of

Literary Trivia

to Don Hauptman,
for his unstinting generosity and insight

to Mattias Lederer,
my fellow English major

to my Haverford College English professors,
who helped me to discover who I am
and why I was put on this planet

Praise for Richard Lederer

Richard Lederer has done it again—another delightful, witty, and hugely absorbing celebration of the English language. Is there no stopping this man? – Bill Bryson, author of *The Mother Tongue*

Richard Lederer is to wordplay what John Philip Sousa is to marches. – Rod L. Evans, author of *Tyrannosaurus Lex*

Richard Lederer ought to be declared a national treasure. No one has more fun with the English language. – *Richmond Times Dispatch*

Also by Richard Lederer

Adventures of a Verbivore
Amazing Words
American Trivia (with Caroline McCullagh)
American Trivia Quiz Book (with Caroline McCullagh)
Anguished English
Animal Cracker Uppers Jr. (with Jim Ertner)
The Ants Are My Friends (with Stan Kegel)
Basic Verbal Skills (with Philip Burnham)
The Big Book of Word Play Crosswords (with Gayle Dean)
The Bride of Anguished English
Building Bridge (with Bo Schambelan and Arnold Fisher)
Challenging Words for Smart People
The Circus of Words
Cleverly Comical Animal Jokes (with Jim Ertner)
Comma Sense (with John Shore)
Crazy English
The Cunning Linguist
Fractured English
Get Thee to a Punnery
The Giant Book of Animal Jokes (with Jim Ertner)
The Gift of Age
Hilarious Holiday Humor (with Stan Kegel)
The Joy of Names
Lederer on Language
A Man of My Words
The Miracle of Language
Monsters Unchained!
More Anguished English
The Play of Words

Presidential Trivia
Pun & Games
The Revenge of Anguished English
Rip Roaring Animal Jokes (with Jim Ertner)
Sleeping Dogs Don't Lay (with Richard Dowis)
Super Funny Animal Jokes (with Jim Ertner)
Theme and Paragraph (with Philip Burnham)
A Treasury for Cat Lovers
A Treasury for Dog Lovers
A Treasury of Christmas Humor
A Treasury of Halloween Humor
A Tribute to Teachers
Wild & Wacky Animal Jokes (with Jim Ertner)
The Word Circus
Word Wizard
The Write Way (with Richard Dowis)

RICHARD LEDERER'S
ULTIMATE BOOK OF
LITERARY TRIVIA

RICHARD LEDERER

Waterside Productions

Printed in the United States of America

First Printing, 2021

ISBN-13: 978-1-954968-46-2 print edition
ISBN-13: 978-1-954968-47-9 ebook edition

Waterside Productions
2055 Oxford Ave
Cardiff, CA 92007
www.waterside.com

TABLE OF CONTENTS

INTRODUCTION

Literature lives. Literature endures. Literature prevails. That's because readers bestow a special kind of life upon people who have existed only in books. Figments though they may be, literary characters can assume a vitality and longevity that pulse more powerfully than flesh and blood.

A woman telephoned an Atlanta library and asked, "Can you please tell me where Scarlett O'Hara is buried?"

The librarian explained, "Scarlett is a fictional character in Margaret Mitchell's novel *Gone With the Wind.*"

"Never mind that," said the caller. "I want to know where she's buried."

For that reader, Scarlett O'Hara had been so alive that now she was dead.

Many years after it first appeared, the publishers of the children's classic *Charlotte's Web* persuaded E.B. White to record his book on tape. So caught had the author become in the web of his arachnid heroine's life that it took nineteen tapings before White could read aloud the passage about Charlotte's death without his voice cracking.

A century earlier, another writer had been deeply affected by the fate of his heroine.

Like most of Charles Dickens's works, *The Old Curiosity Shop* (1841) was published in serial form. The novel won an enthusiastic readership on both sides of the Atlantic, and as interest in the fate of the heroine, Little Nell, grew intense, circulation reached the staggering figure of a hundred thousand. In New York, six thousand people crowded the wharf waiting for the ship carrying the final installment of the story published in *Master Humphrey's Clock* magazine. As the vessel approached, the crowd's impatience grew to such a pitch that they cried out as one to the sailors, "Does Little Nell die?"

Alas, Little Nell did die, and tens of thousands of readers' hearts broke. The often ferocious literary critic Lord Jeffrey was found weeping with his head on his library table. "You'll be sorry to hear," he blubbered to a friend, "that little Nelly, Boz's little Nelly, is dead."

Daniel O'Connell, an Irish M.P., burst out crying, "He should not have killed her," and then, in anguish, hurled the book out of the window of the train in which he was traveling. A diary of the time records another reader lamenting, "The villain! The rascal! The bloodthirsty scoundrel! He killed my little Nell! He killed my sweet little child!"

That "bloodthirsty scoundrel" was himself shattered by the loss of his heroine. In a letter to a friend, Dickens wrote, "I am the wretchedest of the wretched. It [Nell's death] casts the most horrible shadow upon me, and it is as much as I can do to keep moving at all. Nobody will miss her like I shall."

Even more famous than Charlotte and Little Nell is Arthur Conan Doyle's Sherlock Holmes, the world's first consulting detective. These stories have been translated into more than sixty languages, from Arabic to Yiddish. Readers everywhere recognize the intrepid sleuth's deerstalker hat, Inverness cape, calabash pipe, and magnifying glass. It has been said that Sherlock Holmes is the most famous man who never lived.

In December of 1887, Sherlock Holmes came into the world unheralded in *A Study in Scarlet*, published in *Beeton's Christmas Annual*. When, not long after, *The Strand Magazine* began the monthly serialization of the first dozen short stories titled "The Adventures of Sherlock Holmes," the issues sold tens of thousands of copies, and the public clamored for more.

At the height of success, however, the creator wearied of his creation. After writing twenty-four Holmes stories in six years, Doyle yearned for "higher writing" and felt his special calling to be the historical novel. In December 1893, Doyle introduced into "The Final Problem" the arch criminal Professor James Moriarty. In that last story, Holmes and the evil professor wrestle at a cliff's edge in Switzerland. Grasping each other, sleuth and villain plummet to their watery deaths at the foot of the Reichenbach Falls.

With Holmes destroyed, Doyle felt he could turn his authorial eyes to the romantic landscapes of the Middle Ages. He longed to chronicle the clangor of medieval battles, the derring-do of brave knights, and the sighs of lovesick maidens.

But the writer's tour back in time would not be that easily booked. Sherlock Holmes had taken on a life of his own, something larger than the will of his creator. The normally staid, stiff-upper-lipped British public was first bereaved. Even conservative London stockbrokers went to work wearing black armbands in mourning for the loss of their heroic detective. Then the public became outraged. Citizens poured out torrents of letters to editors complaining of Holmes's fate. One woman picketed Doyle's home with a sign branding him a murderer.

The appeals of *The Strand*'s publishers to Doyle's sensibilities and purse went unheeded. For the next eight years, Holmes lay dead at the bottom of the Swiss falls while Doyle branched out into historical fiction, science fiction, horror stories, and medical stories. But he wasn't very good at "higher writing," and it didn't sell well.

Finally, Doyle could resist the pressures from publisher and public no more. In 1903 appeared "The Return of Sherlock Holmes," the series of thirteen stories that brought back Doyle's hero from his watery grave In the Reichenbach Falls, his logical wonders to perform. Readers again queued up by the thousands to buy the monthly installments, and the author continued writing stories of his detective right into 1927. When, in 1930, Arthur Conan Doyle died at age seventy-one, readers around the world mourned his passing. Newspaper cartoons portraying a grieving Sherlock Holmes captured the public's sense of irreparable loss.

Such is the power of mythic literature that the creation has outlived his creator. From all over the world letters and packages still come addressed to "Sherlock Holmes" at 221B Baker Street, his fictional home. Only Santa Claus receives more mail, at least just before Christmas. More movies—well over three hundred of them—have been made about Holmes than about Dracula, Frankenstein, Robin Hood, and James Bond combined. Sherlock Holmes stories written by post-Doylean authors now vastly outnumber the sixty that Doyle produced. More than two hundred and fifty societies in homage to Sherlock Holmes are active in Great Britain, the United States, Australia, Canada, India, and Japan.

However many times the progenitor tried to finish off his hero, by murder or retirement or flat refusal to write any more adventures, the Great Detective lives, vigilant and deductive as ever, protecting us from the evils that lurk in the very heart of our so-called civilization. Sherlock Holmes has never died. Readers around the world simply won't let him.

If you have read this far in this Introduction, you are almost certainly a person for whom the people who live in books are very much alive. I aim to amuse and entertain you with games and quizzes that test your literary literacy. I've constructed the posers in these pages for people like you who love to read. As with any true challenge, however, some of the questions can be answered easily, while others will cause head-scratching among even the most bookish.

Don't get your knickers in a twist if you don't know the answer to many of the questions. You'll learn a lot by reading those answers and adding them to your literary knowledge.

I wrote this *Ultimate Book* of *Literary Trivia* to show just how much fun the study of great—and sometimes more-popular-than-great—literature can be. I expect that you will learn of or be reminded of some of the greatest literature in the English language, along with a selection of foreign classics. In these pages you'll find the classic authors and works as well as modern and contemporary writers, with women and minorities well represented. Ultimately, you may be inspired to read or reread some of the masterpieces presented along the way.

In responding to the games in this book, you may solve fewer than half the challenges on your first try, but you will find that insights into additional answers come to you in sudden flashes when you return to the fun a second or third time. Most readers will play the games as a species of solitaire; I invite you to grapple with the quizzes with other book lovers, if that will add to your social and intellectual pleasure. You, dear reader, are the one in charge.

Benjamin Franklin was a guest at a Paris dinner party when a question was posed: What condition of man most deserves pity? Each guest presented an example of a miserable situation. When Franklin's turn came, he responded, "A lonesome man on a rainy day who does not know how to read." As a member of that happy and privileged band, known as bibliophiles, you will never be lonely. Forevermore you have the company and conversation of thousands of men and women, ancient and contemporary, learned and light, who have set their humanity to paper and sculpted language into literature.

richardhlederer@gmail.com
verbivore.com

A Book Lover's Profile

While many fabrics are colored or printed after they are woven, wool is sometimes dyed before it's woven into cloth. The color of that wool is through-and-through and impossible to remove completely. So when we say someone is a "dyed-in-the-wool" conservative, liberal, environmentalist, animal-rights supporter, Yankees fan, etc., we mean that their beliefs are steadfast and permanent.

You know you're a dyed-in-the-wool book lover if you were that kid who got excited when your teacher asked the class to read silently for a half hour. At home, if you got sent to your room as punishment, you laughed to yourself because that meant an opportunity to be alone, in peace, with a book in your hands and a smile on your face.

When you were little, books were your best friends in the world—and they still are. You know the characters in novels better than you know real people. You yearn to live in the worlds you read about, and you wish you could go on adventures with the people in them. You dream about following The Yellow Brick Road leading to The Emerald City, and you fantasize about leaping inside your wardrobe and traveling to Narnia.

When you're between books, you feel lost—until you open the next one. You experience distress when you are somewhere without a book, a magazine, a newspaper or at least a scrap of paper to read. You know that reading a book is like life renewing itself. And you know that the book is always, always, always better than the movie.

The stack of books on your night table resembles the beginning of a Jenga game.

When you are reading a good book, you sometimes forget to eat or sleep. On a "must-finish" night, you fall asleep with a book still in your hands. The bags under your eyes are not from a kinetic social life but from staying up reading into the wee hours.

When you work out, you choose only the machines that let you read while you're sweating. You can't figure out what people who go to the beach without a book do there. You spend the majority of your vacation time reading, and that includes your honeymoon.

You've read so many books that people don't dare buy them for you anymore. Instead, they give you book-related gift cards. And one of your rapturous joys is when a friend actually reads a book you have recommended—and loves it!

Bookstores are your favorite places. No matter where you are or what you're there for, if you come upon a bookstore, you have to go inside and browse. Three hours later, you emerge with a stack of books in your hands. You can't buy happiness but you can buy books, and that's pretty much the same thing.

AUTHORS

AUTHORIAL ANECDOTES

Henry David Thoreau, who wrote *Walden,* helped runaway slaves escape to Canada and became one of the first Americans to speak in defense of John Brown. When Thoreau spent a day in jail for acting on the dictates of his conscience, he was visited by friend Ralph Waldo Emerson.

Emerson asked, "Henry, why are you here?"

Thoreau answered, "Waldo, why are you *not* here?"

Within the brief compass of a biographical incident we can sometimes catch and crystallize the essence of a person's character.

Here are some colorful episodes from the lives of famous authors, each of whom you are asked to identify:

1. When he was ninety years of age, this Greek tragedian was brought before a court of law by his sons, who sought to have him declared senile and thus incompetent to manage his estate. In his own defense, the playwright read aloud passages from his *Oedipus at Colonus,* which he had recently completed but not yet staged. The jury confirmed his competency, chastised his sons, and escorted him home as an honor.

2. President Abraham Lincoln took this abolitionist author of *Uncle Tom's Cabin* by the hand and said, "So this is the little lady who made this big war."

3. This British writer's rags-to-riches life was more remarkable than any of his sentimental stories. Born into an impoverished family and having worked as a child laborer in a London blacking

factory, he became, at the age of twenty-five, the most popular author in England.

4. Unemployed and living on state benefits, this single mother wrote much of her first novel sitting in local Edinburgh cafes or banging away on a manual typewriter in her sister's home. That first book in her series was rejected by twelve publishers before being accepted by Bloomsbury Publishing—and only then because the chairman's eight-year-old daughter insisted on it. By the time she had completed six of the seven books in her projected series, she was named "the greatest living British writer"—and she certainly became by far the richest.

5. Born a slave on a Virginia plantation in 1856, this author of the *Up From Slavery* rose to become a leading intellectual of the nineteenth and early twentieth century, founder of Tuskegee Normal and Industrial Institute, and advisor to Presidents Theodore Roosevelt and William Howard Taft.

6. This reclusive American writer was depicted in W.P. Kinsella's novel *Shoeless Joe*. When the subject threatened to sue, he was replaced in the film version, titled *Field of Dreams,* by a fictitious writer named Terrence Mann, who was portrayed by James Earl Jones.

7. This writer, critic, and humorist once arrived simultaneously at a narrow doorway with the playwright, journalist, and politician Clare Boothe Luce.

"Age before beauty," said Mrs. Luce, stepping aside.

"Pearls before swine," purred our writer as she glided through the doorway.

8. Born a slave in Maryland and escaping in 1838, this powerful orator became the leading African American in the abolitionist movement. He recruited black soldiers to fight in the Civil War and ultimately produced three autobiographies.

9. At the height of this British writer's popularity, he is said to have earned about a dollar a word. This inspired a certain autograph hound, who had been unsuccessful in obtaining the great man's signature, to try again. He sent off a letter that he was sure

would produce the desired result: "I see you get $1 a word for your writing. I enclose a check for $1. Please send me a sample." The writer replied by postcard—unsigned: "Thanks."

10. In less than nine years, this London man of letters almost single-handedly produced the first authoritative dictionary of the English language, a feat that took academy committees in France and Italy decades to create similar dictionaries in their languages.

11. This politically active English poet became completely blind at the age of forty-five and afterward wrote a sonnet titled "On His Blindness" and the epic poem *Paradise Lost.*

12. This English romantic poet fell asleep under the influence of opium and dreamt a complete vision of a poem, "Kubla Khan." When he awoke, he immediately set to writing out his fantasy but was interrupted by "a person on business from Porlock" and was never able to finish the work.

13. The poet Lord Byron challenged a group of his friends to create their own ghost stories. From that challenge came the tale *Frankenstein,* written by this twenty-one-year-old wife of another romantic poet.

14. When the first edition of this American poet's collection of poems appeared in 1855, the *Boston Intelligencer* said in its review: "The author should be kicked out from all decent society as below the level of the brute. He must be some escaped lunatic raving in pitiable delirium." The collection went through nine more editions and gained a large, enthusiastic readership in the United States and England.

15. Only seven of this New England woman's poems were published during her lifetime, and she left instructions that all of her manuscripts be destroyed. Today, she and her contemporary in the question above are the two most widely read and influential American poets of the nineteenth century.

16. This New England writer had 706 of one of his unsold books returned to him by a book dealer. In a journal entry he wrote, "I

now have a library of nearly nine hundred volumes, over seven hundred of which I wrote myself."

17. This American humorist and member of the famed Algonquin Round Table once quipped, "It took me fifteen years to discover that I had no talent for writing, but I couldn't give it up because by that time I was too famous."

18. Worn down by poverty, this unknown Scottish poet resolved to emigrate to Jamaica in 1786. To finance the journey, he gathered together some of his poems in a thin volume. The small collection took Scotland by storm, and the young man went on to become his country's national poet.

19. This London pre-Romantic poet was also a painter, engraver, and spiritual visionary. He possessed eidetic sight, a quality that allowed him to see visions as well as imagine them. When he was but a child, he claimed to have seen the prophet Ezekiel in a tree. His vivid engravings designed to accompany his poems made him the world's first multimedia artist.

20. As a young cadet, this American writer was expelled from West Point for reporting to a march wearing nothing but white gloves.

21. This British writer showed his first novel, *The White Peacock*, to his coal-miner father. After struggling through half a page, the father asked, "And what dun they gie thee for that, lad?"

"Fifty pounds, Father," the son answered.

"Fifty pounds!" exclaimed the dumbfounded father. "Fifty pounds! An' tha's niver done a day's hard work in thy life!"

22. When he was a young busboy in a Washington, D.C., hotel, this American poet left a packet of his poems next to the poet Vachel Lindsay's plate. Lindsay helped to launch the young man's career, and the busboy became the leading figure in the Harlem Renaissance.

23. When a popular Jazz Age American novelist remarked to another famous writer that "the rich are very different from you

andme," the latter replied, "Yes, they have more money." Name the two authors.

24. *I Know Why the Caged Bird Sings* was the first of seven memoirs this African American author wrote. She went on to become the first black female cable-car conductor in San Francisco, a star of the New York Theater, a foreign service aide in Ghana, a magazine editor in Cairo, and the first African American woman to direct a major feature film.

25. When this Russian writer's first novel was well received in 1846, he joined a revolutionary group that was infiltrated by the authorities. Together with several associates, he was tried and sentenced to be shot. The execution was a cruel hoax, and, at the very last minute, the sentence was commuted to years of hard labor in Siberia. Ten years later he returned to St. Petersburg and became one of the greatest of all Russian authors.

26. Author of the wildly popular *Vampire Chronicles*, this woman was born with the unusual name Howard Allen Frances O'Brien.

27. A nineteen-month-old girl lay dying in a London hospital. Her condition baffled the doctors until a nurse noted that the patient's symptoms were remarkably like those of an infant in the detective novel *Pale Horse*. The nurse's suggestion that the patient could have thallium poisoning was confirmed by tests. Given proper treatment, the baby recovered. Who was the famous author of *Pale Horse*?

28. This conjurer of animal fables is said to have been a deformed black slave who lived in the sixth century B.C. According to tradition, he used his fables to bolster his arguments and, ultimately, to win his freedom

29. The science-fiction stories of this French author were called "dreams come true." So prophetic was his description of a periscope in *Twenty Thousand Leagues Under the Sea* that a few years later the actual inventor of the instrument was refused permission for an original patent.

30. After reaching forty, this housewife and mother of five began writing her first book in the *Earth's Children* fictional saga. The series has gone on to become one of the best-selling in publishing history.

31. This American poet was asked to compose a poem and read it at John F. Kennedy's inauguration in 1961. When the sun's glare prevented him from reading the poem at the occasion, he instead recited "The Gift Outright" from memory.

32. In writing her novel *Beloved*, about the horrors of slavery, this Nobel Prize for Literature winner researched historical documents and artifacts. She became appalled by the "bit" that masters, as punishment, inserted in the mouths of slaves.

33. This African American slave mastered English in sixteen months after having been conscripted to the United Statesand, as a young woman. With the appearance of her small collection of poetry, she became the first African living in the British colonies to be a published author and the second American woman to author a book of verse.

34. In the mid 1980s, this small-town lawyer and Mississippi state legislator would fill his time between court hearings and meetings writing legal thrillers. His first novel sold fewer than five thousand copies. Then he wrote *The Firm*.

35. This southern author of *The Help* revealed in an interview, "I was scared, a lot of the time, that I was crossing a terrible line, writing in the voice of a black person. I don't presume to think that I know what it really felt like to be a black woman in Mississippi, especially in the 1960s. I don't think it is something any white woman on the other end of a black woman's paycheck could ever truly understand."

Answers

1. Sophocles 2. Harriet Beecher Stowe 3. Charles Dickens 4. J.K. Rowling 5. Booker T. Washington

6. J.D. Salinger 7. Dorothy Parker 8. Frederick Douglass 9. Rudyard Kipling 10. Samuel Johnson

11. John Milton 12. Samuel Taylor Coleridge 13. Mary Wollstonecraft Shelley 14. Walt Whitman 15. Emily Dickinson

16. Henry David Thoreau 17. Robert Benchley 18. Robert Burns 19. William Blake 20. Edgar Allan Poe

21. D.H. Lawrence 22. Langston Hughes 23. F. Scott Fitzgerald and Ernest Hemingway 24. Maya Angelou 25. Fyodor Dostoevsky

26. Anne Rice 27. Agatha Christie 28. Aesop 29. Jules Verne 30. Jean Auel

31. Robert Frost 32. Toni Morrison 33. Phyllis Wheatley 34. John Grisham 35. Kathryn Stockett

AUTHOR! AUTHOR! AUTHOR!

On a February day in 1892, Charles Buzzell, who had lain unconscious for nine days without food and water, was nearly dead by the time he got to St. Vincent's Hospital. Doctors battled the odds to keep him alive—and won.

The heroism of the medical staff so impressed Buzzell's married sister that when she gave birth to a daughter not long thereafter, she honored the institution by making it part of the baby's name. That's how poet Edna St. Vincent Millay came to be named—in the cadence of dactylic trimeter!—for a New York hospital.

Edna St. Vincent Millay is a trinomial, that is, a person who is best known by three names. To gain a glimpse into a time when trinomials were more in fashion, have a look at the middle names of dead poets and other writers who were best known by three names.

Identify the first and last name of each writer.

1. _____ Allan _____
2. _____ Anne _____
3. _____ Arlington _____
4. _____ Barrett _____
5. _____ Bashevis _____
6. _____ Beecher _____
7. _____ Bernard _____
8. _____ Boothe _____
9. _____ Butler _____
10. _____ Bysshe _____
11. _____ Carlos _____
12. _____ Carol _____
13. _____ Chandler _____
14. _____ Christian _____
15. _____ Clarke _____
16. _____ Conan _____
17. _____ David _____
18. _____ Dean _____
19. _____ Fenimore _____
20. _____ Foster _____
21. _____ Greenleaf _____
22. _____ Hong _____
23. _____ Ingalls _____
24. _____ Jeter _____

25. ____ Kearns ____	38. ____ Redmon ____
26. ____ Kinnan ____	39. ____ Rice ____
27. ____ Lawrence ____	40. ____ Russell ____
28. ____ Louis ____	41. ____ Stanley ____
29. ____ Mae ____	42. ____ Taylor ____
30. ____ Makepeace ____	43. ____ Vincent ____
31. ____ Maria ____	44. ____ Wadsworth ____
32. ____ May ____	45. ____ Waldo ____
33. ____ Monk ____	46. ____ Ward ____
34. ____ Neale ____	47. ____ Weldon ____
35. ____ Orne ____	48. ____ Wendell ____
36. ____ Penn ____	49. ____ Whitcomb ____
37. ____ Prawer ____	50. ____ Wollstonecraft ____

Answers

1. Edgar Allan Poe (Poe's middle name may be the most misspelled in the canon.) 2. Katherine Anne Porter 3. Edwin Arlington Robinson 4. Elizabeth Barrett Browning 5. Isaac Bashevis Singer

6. Harriet Beecher Stowe 7. George Bernard Shaw 8. Clare Booth Luce 9. William Butler Yeats 10. Percy Bysshe Shelley

11. William Carlos Williams 12. Joyce Carol Oates 13. Joel Chandler Harris 14. Hans Christian Andersen 15. Clement Clarke Moore

16. Arthur Conan Doyle 17. Henry David Thoreau 18. William Dean Howells 19. James Fenimore Cooper 20. David Foster Wallace

21. John Greenleaf Whittier 22. Maxine Hong Kingston 23. Laura Ingalls Wilder 24. Sena Jeter Naslund 25. Doris Kearns Goodwin

26. Marjorie Kinnan Rawlings 27. Ernest Lawrence Thayer 28. Robert Louis Stevenson 29. Rita Mae Brown 30. William Makepeace Thackeray

31. Erich Maria Remarque 32. Louisa May Alcott 33. Sue Monk Kidd 34. Zora Neale Hurston 35. Sarah Orne Jewett

36. Robert Penn Warren 37. Ruth Prawer Jhabvala 38. Jessie Redmon Fauset 39. Edgar Rice Burroughs 40. James Russell Lowell

41. Erle Stanley Gardner 42. Samuel Taylor Coleridge 43. Stephen Vincent Benét 44. Henry Wadsworth Longfellow 45. Ralph Waldo Emerson

46. Julia Ward Howe or Henry Ward Beecher 47. James Weldon Johnson 48. Oliver Wendell Holmes 49. James Whitcomb Riley 50. Mary Wollstonecraft Shelley

LETTER-PERFECT WRITERS

Other writers prefer to be known by their initials rather than their full names.

Take the initiative and match the writerly initials in the left-hand column with the last names in the right-hand column:

1. A.A.	Andrews
2. A.E.	Annie Proulx
3. C.S.	Auden
4. E.	Barrie
5. E.B	Chesterton
6. E.E.	Cummings
7. E.L.	Doctorow
8. E.M.	Du Bois
9. F.	Eliot
10. G.K.	Forster
11. H.G.	Frank Baum
12. H.L.	Henry
13. H.P.	Hinton
14. J.D.	Housman
15. J.K.	James
16. J.M.	Lewis
17. J.R.R.	Lovecraft
18. L.	Mencken
19. O.	Milne
20. P.D.	Perelman

21. P.G.	Rowling
22. P.L.	Salinger
23. R.L.	Scott Fitzgerald
24. S.E.	Somerset Maugham
25. S.J.	Stein
26. T.S.	Tolkien
27. V.C.	Travers
28. W.	Wells
29. WE.B.	White
30. W.H.	Wodehouse

Answers

1. A.A. Milne 2. A.E. Housman 3. C.S. Lewis 4. E. Annie Proulx 5. E.B. White

6. E.E. Cummings 7. E.L. Doctorow 8. E.M. Forster 9. F. Scott Fitzgerald 10. G.K. Chesterton

11. H.G. Wells 12. H.L. Mencken 13. H.P. Lovecraft 14. J.D. Salinger 15. J.K. Rowling

16. J.M. Barrie 17. J.R.R. Tolkien 18. L. Frank Baum 19. O. Henry 20. P.D. James

21. P.G. Wodehouse 22. P.L. Travers 23. R.L. Stein 24. S.E. Hinton 25. S.J. Perelman

26. T.S. Eliot 27. V.C. Andrews 28. W. Somerset Maugham 29. W.E.B. Du Bois 30. W.H. Auden

PEN-ULTIMATE NAMES

The authors of *Alice's Adventures in Wonderland, Silas Marner,* and *Nineteen Eighty-Four* have something in common besides being British. They are all better known by their pseudonyms, or pen names, than by their birth-certificate names.

It's hard to imagine why a writer who goes to the trouble of scratching out a work of art would want to be known by another identity. On the other hand, if you were born Amandine Lucie Aurore Dupin, Jacques Anatole François Thibault, or Aleksey Maximovich Peshkov, you might adopt the nom de plume of George Sand, Anatole France, or Maxim Gorky. And, if it's efficiency you seek, it's obvious that Moliere, Voltaire, and Stendhal are considerably more compact than Jean-Baptiste Poquelin, Francois-Marie Arouet, and Marie Henri Beyle.

As a barefoot boy sitting on the banks of the Mississippi River, Samuel Langhorne Clemens watched stern-wheeler boats churning the muddy waters, and he heard the leadsmen sounding the depth of the river by calling out to the captains, "By the deep six... by the mark five... by the deep four... by the mark three." When the river bottom was only two fathoms, or twelve feet down, he would hear the lusty cry "by the mark twain." After he left the Mississippi, and after various careers as a riverboat pilot, prospector, and printer, Sam Clemens, now a journalist, contributed an article to the *Nevada Territorial Enterprise* on February 3, 1863, and signed it with a new name—Mark Twain.

The British poet laureate Robert Southey admonished a girl who had written him asking if she had any chance of becoming a great writer. "Literature cannot be the business of a woman's life," he replied, "and it ought not to be. The more she is engaged in her proper duties, the less leisure she will have for it, even as an accomplishment and a recreation. To those duties you have not yet been called, and when you are, you will be less eager for celebrity."

The aspiring author was Charlotte Brontë.

Have you ever heard of the Bell brothers? No. But as a reader of this book you have heard of the three Brontë sisters—Charlotte, Emily, and Anne, who were engaged in a friendly scribbling rivalry. But as Southey's sneer indicates, in nineteenth century England female writers were thought to be improper and unmarketable, so the three gifted authors donned masculine pseudonyms—Currier Bell (Charlotte), Ellis Bell (Emily), and Acton Bell (Anne).

Here are brief biographies of twenty famous writers who made the change. From the information supplied, identify each pseudonym.

1. Eric Arthur Blair wrote a long fable about a society in which some animals are more equal than others. In 1948 he published a novel about a nightmarish society of the future, one in which everybody had a Big Brother.

2. After J.K. Rowling created her colossally successful Harry Potter series, she wrote crime fiction under the name _____.

3. In March 1836, what has been described as the most successful writing career in history was launched with the publication of *The Posthumous Papers of the Pickwick Club*. The author, of course, was Charles Dickens. In 1833, when he was only twenty-one, Dickens began contributing stories and essays to magazines and published them pseudonymously in a collection called *Sketches by* _____.

4. Charles Lutwidge Dodgson was fascinated with words, logic, and little girls. Out of these interests he fashioned a wonderland of characters—Humpty Dumptys, Jabberwocks, Mad Hatters, and White Rabbits.

5. Famous for her novels describing life in nineteenth century England, including *Adam Bede, Silas Marner,* and *Middlemarch,* Mary Ann Evans adopted a masculine pen name, by George.

6. He meant what he said, and he said what he meant, and his books have pleased children one hundred percent. Theodore Seuss Geisel conjured up and drew creatures that now live and move and have their beings in the imaginations of generations of children.

7. Convicted of embezzlement, William Sydney Porter spent almost four years in prison, where he began his career as an immensely popular writer of short stories. Most of his tales are about life in New York and are marked by surprise endings.

8. Late in life, after a long career as a veterinary surgeon, James Alfred Wight wrote two dozen books that communicated his profound affection for animals. The titles of four of those books are taken from a hymn that begins, "All things bright and beautiful, all creatures great and small."

9. Jozef Korzeniowski was born in Poland and grew up speaking no English until he was seventeen, yet he became one of the greatest stylists ever to use the English language. A sailor as a youth, Korzeniowski is most famous for his stories and novels of the sea.

10. Chloe Ardelia Wofford became a writer of novels, short fiction, and children's literature largely about the realities of the African American experience. In 1993, she became the first black woman from any country to win the Nobel Prize for Literature.

11. An unpublished Atlanta writer named Peggy Marsh submitted an incomplete manuscript that filled a large suitcase. The title of the novel was to be *Tomorrow Is Another Day,* and its heroine was to be called Pansy. After a great number of changes, including the title and name of the heroine, the book was published in 1936 and quickly became an all-time best-seller, inspiring a blockbuster movie.

12. Russian-born Yiddish author Solomon Rabinowitz took his pen name from a Hebrew expression meaning "peace be unto you."

13. British novelist and critic John B. Wilson is most famous for *A Clockwork Orange*. His works often combine word play and a grim view of life.

14. Baroness Karen Blixen, a Danish author who wrote primarily in English, managed a coffee plantation in British East Africa. She is best known for her tales and autobiography drawn from her African experiences.

15. For many years, Manfred Lee and his cousin Frederic Dannay functioned as one author, an eccentric bookworm who allegedly wrote about his adventures as a detective.

16. As a little girl, Marguerite Annie Johnson was nicknamed Maya, short for "mya sister." After a brief marriage to a Greek sailor named Tosh Angelos, she combined her childhood nickname with a form of her ex-husband's name to create her pseudonym.

17. Daniel Handler is best known for his children's books, especially *A Series of Unfortunate Events*, published under a fanciful pseudonym.

18. What a wicked sense of humor this founding father had. In 1722, Benjamin Franklin submitted a series of "charming" letters to the *New-England Courant*, one of the first very American newspapers. Franklin purported to be a middle-aged widow.

19. Mega-selling author Stephen King wrote several books under a pseudonym because his publisher felt he was turning out too many titles and saturating the market.

20. Hector Hugh Munro was killed in action during World War I. He left behind him the charming, often biting short stories to which he signed a pseudonym borrowed from *The Rubaiyat*

Answers

1. George Orwell 2. Robert Galbraith 3. Boz 4. Lewis Carroll 5. George Eliot

6. Dr. Seuss 7. O. Henry 8. James Herriot 9. Joseph Conrad 10. Toni Morrison

11. Margaret Mitchell 12. Sholem Aleichem 13. Anthony Burgess 14. Isak Dinesen 15. Ellery Queen

16. Maya Angelou 17. Lemony Snicket 18. Silence Dogood (I'll bet you didn't get that one.) 19. Richard Bachman 20. Saki

Also Known As...

A nickname is a substitution of a given name or surname for the purposes of affection, ridicule, or group identity. The word *nickname* boasts an ancient history. It first appeared in the 1300s in the English language as "an eke name," *eke* related to "augment" and meaning "also, additional." In the early 1500s, someone divided the words in the wrong way, and "an eke name" became "a nekename." From there it was only a short leap to "nickname." The spelling and meaning have stayed the same ever since. (*A napron, a numpire,* and *a nuncle* underwent a similar makeover.)

Match each nickname with each original name:

1. The Bard of Avon	Aristotle
2. The Bard of Rydall Mount	Geoffrey Chaucer
3. The Belle of Amherst	Emily Dickinson
4. Darwin's Bulldog	Ralph Waldo Emerson
5. The Father of English Literature	Ernest Hemingway
6. The Good Gray Poet	Homer
7. The Lexicographer	Thomas Henry Huxley
8. The Mantuan Swan	Samuel Johnson
9. Papa	Alexander Pope
10. The Patriot Dean	Walter Scott
11. The Sage of Concord	William Shakespeare
12. The Stargirite	Jonathan Swift

13. The Swan of Meander   Virgil
14. The Wasp of Twickenham   Walt Whitman
15. The Wizard of the North   William Wordsworth

Answers

1. William Shakespeare 2. William Wordsworth 3. Emily Dickinson 4. Thomas Henry Huxley 5. Geoffrey Chaucer

6. Walt Whitman 7. Samuel Johnson 8. Virgil 9. Ernest Hemingway 10. Jonathan Swift

11. Ralph Waldo Emerson 12. Aristotle 13. Homer 14. Alexander Pope 15. Walter Scott

Now step right up to a brain-powdering game of anagrams. An anagram is a rearrangement of all the letters in a word or sentence to make a new and penetrating word or sentence. For centuries, letter-ers have been anagramming the names of the famous and infamous, including writers.

Match each author below with his or her anagram.

1. Adeline Virginia Woolf   ART, BEAUTY WILL SMILE.
2. Agatha Christie   A CAR TUMBLES.
3. Albert Camus   A VERY HIDDEN AUTHOR
4. Beatrix Potter   CHEER SICK LANDS.
5. Charles Dickens   DARE SHUN ISLAM
6. Charlotte Brontë   DELOUSE MY ALLEGORIC ART.
7. Ernest Hemingway   EXTRA-BRIT POET
8. Gertrude Stein   WISEST MEN SEE IN ALL.
9. Henry David Thoreau   HE'LL DO IN MELLOW VERSE.
10. Henry Wadsworth Longfellow   I, A LOVING WIFE; I, LEONARD
11. Miguel Cervantes de Saavedra   I LACE WORDS.
12. Oliver Wendell Holmes   I LOVE ART.
13. Oscar Wilde   IS A THEATRIC HAG

14. Ralph Waldo Emerson	LAST SCOT WRITER
15. Richard Lederer	LET NO BROTHER ACT.
16. Salman Rushdie	LITOTES (also TOILETS)
17. Samuel Taylor Coleridge	PERSON WHOM ALL READ
18. Sir Walter Scott	RIDDLER REACHER
19. Truman Capote	TEACUP MATRON
20. Tennessee Williams	URGED INTEREST
21. T.S. Eliot	WE ALL MAKE HIS PRAISE.
22. Voltaire	WHERE'S MY NEAT GIN?
23. William Butler Yeats	WORLD WITH WARM SOIL
24. William Shakespeare	WON HALF THE NEW WORLD'S GLORY
25. William Wordsworth	GAVE US DAMNED CLEVER SATIRE

Answers

1. I, A LOVING WIFE; I, LEONARD 2. IS A THEATRIC HAG 3. A CAR TUMBLES. 4. EXTRA-BRIT POET 5. CHEER SICK LANDS

6. LET NO BROTHER ACT. 7. WHERE'S MY NEAT GIN? 8. URGED INTEREST 9. A VERY HIDDEN AUTHOR 10. WON HALF THE NEW WORLD'S GLORY

11. GAVE US A DAMNED CLEVER SATIRE 12. HE'LL DO IN MELLOW VERSE. 13. I LACE WORDS. 14. PERSON WHOM ALL READ 15. RIDDLER REACHER

16. DARE SHUN ISLAM 17. DELOUSE MY ALLEGORIC ART. 18. LAST SCOT WRITER 19. TEACUP MATRON 20. WISEST MEN SEE IN ALL.

21. LITOTES (also TOILETS) 22. I LOVE ART. 23. ART, BEAUTY WILL SMILE. 24. WE ALL MAKE HIS PRAISE. 25. WORLD WITH WARM SOIL

OUR WRITERLY PRESIDENTS

U lysses S. Grant claimed to smoke seven to ten cigars a day. When word got out of the president's love of stogies, people sent him more than ten thousand boxes of cigars. Grant finished his two-hundred-thousand word *Personal Memoirs* only a few days before his death from throat cancer, so he never saw the work published. Grant's cancer and the forfeiture of his military pension when he became president bankrupted him, but his popular autobiography ultimately brought in $450,000 for his family.

Personal Memoirs: Ulysses S. Grant remains one of the finest accounts of the Civil War ever written. The book was published with the help of his friend Mark Twain in 1885, the same year that Twain came out with *The Adventures of Huckleberry Finn.*

John Adams, our second president, sometimes wrote under the pseudonym Humphrey Ploughjogger. In four articles in the *Boston Gazette,* Adams employed that pen name in fierce opposition to the despised Stamp Act.

Herbert Hoover wrote nineteen books, including one called *Fishing for Fun and to Wash Your Soul.*

John F. Kennedy is the only president to have received a Pulitzer Prize, for his book *Profiles in Courage.*

Jimmy Carter authored thirty-three books, many of which have been best sellers. He wrote most of his works after his presidency and some with his wife Rosalynn as co-author. In 2003, Carter wrote a novel *The Hornet's Nest*, a fictional story of the Revolutionary War in the South. He was the only presidential novelist, until Bill

Clinton teamed with mega-seller James Patterson to author *The President Is Missing* (2018).

Our most writerly president is Theodore Roosevelt, whose piston energy generated forty-seven books, including *The Rough Riders* (1899), a best-selling memoir before the author became a popular president.

Using the hints provided, name the authors in chief who wrote each of the following books.

1. *Rules of Civility & Decent Behavior in Company & Conversation* (1748)

Rule 1 might be "Don't lie about chopping down cherry trees."

2. *Letters on Freemasonry* (1833)

This author's dad was also a president and author.

3. *The Autobiography of _____* (1860)

This president's autobiography was chock full of the author's policy statements from his debates with Stephen Douglas. The first edition sold out in a blink and propelled him to the highest office in the land.

4. *Fireside Chats*

Radio broadcasts that aired 1933-1944.

5. *Crusade in Europe* (1948)

World War II experiences.

6. *The Vantage Point: Perspectives of the Presidency, 1963-1969* (1971)

The author was the fourth president to become chief executive after the assassination of his president.

7. *A Time to Heal* (1979)

Healing after the resignation of the author's predecessor.

8. *The Art of the Deal* (1987)

The author is the quintessential wheeler dealer.

9. *In the Arena: A Memoir of Victory, Defeat, and Renewal* (1990)

A president who resigned reflects on his long career in the political arena.

10. *An American Life* (1991)

Opening line: "If I'd gotten the job I wanted at Montgomery Ward, I suppose I would never have left Illinois."

11. *My Life* (2005)

More than a thousand pages, this is the heftiest of presidential memoirs.

12. *The Audacity of Hope* (2006)

This book helped a freshman senator ascend to the presidency for two terms.

Answers

1. George Washington 2. John Quincy Adams 3. Abraham Lincoln 4. Franklin Roosevelt 5. Dwight D. Eisenhower 6. Lyndon Johnson

7. Gerald Ford 8. Donald Trump 9. Richard Nixon 10. Ronald Reagan 11. Bill Clinton 12. Barack Obama

LIFE CHANGERS

Every so often comes along a book that changes the way we think. In 1946, appeared one of those books, *Baby and Child Care*, by Dr. Benjamin Spock, a pediatrician who studied psychoanalysis and encouraged moms and dads to "Trust yourself. You know more than you think you know."

Baby and Child Care became one of the best-selling books ever and shaped the way baby boomers and subsequent generations of children were brought up. Spock advised parents to treat their children as individuals, to be more flexible and affectionate with them, and to be more diplomatic in discipline. Benjamin Spock is the only man ever to have written a mega-seller, won an Olympic gold medal (1924, in rowing), and run for the United States presidency (1972, for the People's Party).

Using these descriptions of life-altering books, identify each author:

1. The novel *Oliver Twist* (1827) helped bring about improvements in the treatment of indigent children in England.

2. *Uncle Tom's Cabin* (1852) has been recognized as the book that ignited the American Civil War. 3. *The Interpretation of Dreams* (1899) is still in print around the globe since its first appearance in German and remains a major influence on psychiatry and psychology.

4. *The Jungle* (1906) exposed the horrors of the Chicago meat-packing industry. The novel ignited public outrage and

legislation that improved the quality of food processing and working conditions

5. *The Grapes of Wrath* (1939), by a Nobel Prize-winning author, became the most widely read depiction of life in the Great Depression.

6. *Silent Spring* (1962) alerted a large audience to the environmental, animal, and human damage wrought by the indiscriminate use of DDT.

7. *The Feminine Mystique* (1963) showed the world the pervasive dissatisfaction of women with their lives in post World War II society.

8. *Unsafe at Any Speed* (1965) ushered in the modern consumer movement and drove a car from the market.

9. *In Cold Blood* (1966) launched the genre known as "true crime."

10. *Time* magazine called *In the Shadow of Man* (1971) "an instant animal classic" because the book radically changed our view of our closest animal relative, the chimpanzee.

11. *Drawing on the Right Side of the Brain* (1979) exerted a revolutionary influence on how art is taught.

12. *A Brief History of Time* (1988) elucidated for lay readers the origin of the universe, the chronology of the Big Bang, and the cosmology of black holes.

13. This Pulitzer Prize-winning book, *Guns, Germs, and Steel* (1997), provided a new way of looking at Eurasian hegemony in the world.

14. *Fast Food Nation* (2001) shone light on the dark side of the All-American meal and the global influence of the fast-food industry.

15. This U.S. vice president released *An Inconvenient Truth* (2006) in conjunction with a documentary of the same name, raising awareness of global warming.

Answers

1. Charles Dickens 2. Harriet Beecher Stowe 3. Sigmund Freud 4. Upton Sinclair 5. John Steinbeck

6. Rachel Carson 7. Betty Friedan 8. Ralph Nader 9. Truman Capote 10. Jane Goodall

11. Betty Edwards 12. Stephen Hawking 13. Jared Diamond 14. Eric Schlosser 15. Al Gore

LITERARY WORD MAKERS

Authors also change our way of thinking by creating new words and phrases. When we think about inventions, we conjure up visions of the wheel, the sail, and the electric light—artifacts that humankind has not always possessed. Words are such an integral part of our consciousness that we believe that they have always existed, like stones and grass and trees. But words are more like weaving and flint tools. Each new word is inventively spoken or written for the very first time by a particular human being at a particular moment.

Although the identities of most of these wordmakers are lost in the mist of history, we do know who were the creators of a number of neologisms ("new words"). Many of these neologizers are novelists, playwrights, poets, and essayists who are gifted with a keen ear for language, who love to play with words, and who record their fanciful fabrications in print. They change the world by changing the word.

The etymological meaning of *poet* is "maker," and in a very literal sense some of the mightiest of English poets have been the makers of our vocabulary. The first great poet to write in Middle English was Geoffrey Chaucer, who contributed many nouns that end with the French suffix – *tion*, including *attention, duration, fraction,* and *position.*

Edmund Spenser, Chaucer's successor in the imperial line of British epic poets, was the first English writer who self-consciously cobbled new words. From Spenser's allegorical epic, *The Faerie Queene,* issue *blatant, braggadocio, briny, shiny,* and *violin.*

Joining Chaucer and Spenser in the pantheon of epic poets is John Milton. For his lofty and sonorous *Paradise Lost,* Milton needed a name for the hall of the fallen angels. Following the analogy of *pantheon*, Milton welded together *pan*, "all," and *demon*, "devil," to forge *pandemonium*, which literally means "a place of all demons." Because Satan and his company were noisy and mischief-making, the meaning of *pandemonium* has broadened to mean "uproar or tumult." Milton's noble and prolific mind also birthed *all-conquering, dimensionless, earthshaking, impassive, infinitude, lovelorn, sensuous*, and *smooth shaven*, as well as the expression *light fantastic*.

Leaping centuries ahead, we know that *nerd* first appeared in print in 1950 in the Dr. Seuss children's book *If I Ran the Zoo*. Therein, a boy named Gerald McGrew makes a great number of delightfully extravagant claims as to what he would do if he were in charge at the zoo. Among these fanciful schemes is:

> And then just to show them, I'll sail to Ka-Troo
> And bring back an IT-KUTCH, a PREEP, and a PROO,
> A NERKLE, a NERD, and a SEERSUCKER, too!

Beyond single words, here's a select shelf of expressions that entered our vocabulary through twentieth-century literature. Identify each author.

1. "So it goes." *Slaughterhouse-Five*
2. "Not with a bang, but a whimper." "The Hollow Men"
3. "Big Brother is watching you." *Nineteen Eighty-Four*
4. "the perfect storm" *The Perfect Storm*
5. "I have promises to keep." "The Road Not Taken"
6. "Do not go gentle into that good night."
   "Do Not Go Gentle Into That Good Night"
7. "That's some catch, that Catch-22." *Catch-22*

Answers

1. Kurt Vonnegut 2. T.S. Eliot 3. George Orwell 4. Sebastian Junger 5. Robert Frost (both the line and the title) 6. Dylan Thomas 7. Joseph Heller

MOONLIGHTING FOR SIXPENCE

If Samuel Johnson was correct when he thundered that "no man but a blockhead ever wrote except for money," most writers are blockheads. They write for the love, not the money.

The most William Shakespeare ever earned for writing a play was $2,000 in today's money and never made more in a year than $4,000. in today's money. Fortunately, he was part owner of an acting company and owner of some real estate, making him fairly prosperous.

"To coin one's brain into silver," Edgar Allan Poe once wrote, "is to my thinking the hardest job in the world." It took him a year and a half to pry loose his ten-dollar payment from the *New York Mirror* for a poem the paper had printed. That poem was "The Raven."

Ralph Waldo Emerson customarily received five dollars for each lecture he delivered and often had to argue with his sponsors about whether or not the oats for his horse were included in the payment.

Julia Ward Howe received a miserly four dollars from the *Atlantic Monthly* for her enduring and often-sung poem "Battle Hymn of the Republic."

The preternaturally prolific Henry James wrote sardonically to Edith Wharton, "With the proceeds of my last novel, I purchased a small go-cart, or hand-barrow, on which my guests' luggage is wheeled from the station to my house. It needs a coat of paint. With the proceeds of my next novel I shall have it painted."

Because most writers cannot survive solely by their pens, they must often work in other professions, not always to their liking. While writing *Barchester Towers, The Eustace Diamonds,* and almost fifty other novels, Anthony Trollope worked as a British postal official. Each day he rose at 5:30 a.m. and wrote a thousand words an hour for two-and-a-half hours before going to work. During his thirty-three years of service, he invented the street corner mailbox, making him doubly a man of letters.

Eudora Welty wrote about the career of another postal employee, this one a postmaster in Oxford, Mississippi: "Let us imagine that here and now, we're all in the old university post office and living in the Twenties. We've come up to the stamp window to buy a two-cent stamp, but we see nobody there. We knock and then we pound, and then we pound again and there's not a sound back there. So we holler his name, and at last here he is, William Faulkner. We interrupted him. When he should have been putting up the mail and selling stamps at the window up front, he was out of sight in the back writing lyric poems."

When Henry Miller quit his job as a branch manager for Western Union, he vowed never to work for anyone else again. Of his four-and-a-half years of employment he said, "It was a period comparable, for me, to Dostoevsky's stay in Siberia."

The authors listed below often earned daily bread by means other than their pens.

Match each writer with the profession he or she followed:

1. Maya Angelou	accountant
2. Matthew Arnold	ad writer
3. Honoré de Balzac	apothecary-surgeon
4. Ambrose Bierce	architect
5. John Bunyan	attorney
6. Lewis Carroll	bank teller
7. Daniel Defoe	Civil War general
8. Charles Dickens	customs house surveyor
9. John Donne	dentist
10. Arthur Conan Doyle	diplomat
11. Paul Laurence Dunbar	doctor
12. Zane Grey	elevator operator

13. Thomas Hardy	entomologist
14. Nathaniel Hawthorne	fry cook
15. O. Henry	imperial policeman
16. James Herriot	inspector of schools
17. Eric Hoffer	insurance attorney
18. Oliver Wendell Holmes	Jesuit priest
19. Gerard Manley Hopkins	law clerk
20. A.E. Housman	lens grinder
21. Langston Hughes	librarian
22. Washington Irving	longshoreman
23. Samuel Johnson	mathematician
24. John Keats	Napoleonic dragoon
25. Rudyard Kipling	newspaper columnist
26. Charles Lamb	newspaper editor
27. Jack London	newspaper reporter
28. Herman Melville	ophthalmologist
29. John Milton	patent office clerk
30. Marianne Moore	pediatrician
31. Vladimir Nabokov	pencil maker
32. George Orwell	pilot
33. Samuel Richardson	police detective
34. Antoine de Saint-Exupery	political pamphleteer
35. Dorothy L. Sayers	preacher
36. Walter Scott	printer
37. Benedict Spinoza	professor of Anglo-Saxon
38. Stendhal	prospector
39. Wallace Stevens	schoolmaster
40. Henry David Thoreau	seaman
41. J.R.R. Tolkien	steamboat pilot
42. Mark Twain	tinker
43. Lew Wallace	tobacco merchant
44. Joseph Wambaugh	veterinarian
45. William Carlos Williams	waiter

Answers

1. Maya Angelou – fry cook 2. Matthew Arnold – inspector of schools 3. Honoré de Balzac – law clerk 4. Ambrose Bierce – newspaper columnist 5. John Bunyan – tinker 6. Lewis Carroll – mathematician 7. Daniel Defoe – tobacco merchant 8. Charles Dickens – newspaper reporter 9. John Donne – preacher 10. Arthur Conan Doyle – ophthalmologist

11. Paul Laurence Dunbar – elevator operator 12. Zane Grey – dentist 13. Thomas Hardy – architect 14. Nathaniel Hawthorne – customs house surveyor 15. O. Henry – bank teller

16. James Herriot – veterinarian 17. Eric Hoffer – longshoreman 18. Oliver Wendell Holmes – doctor 19. Gerard Manley Hopkins – Jesuit priest 20. A.E. Housman – patent office clerk

21. Langston Hughes – waiter 22. Washington Irving – diplomat 23. Samuel Johnson – schoolmaster 24. John Keats – apothecary-surgeon 25. Rudyard Kipling – newspaper editor

26. Charles Lamb – accountant 27. Jack London – prospector 28. Herman Melville – seaman 29. John Milton – political pamphleteer 30. Marianne Moore – librarian

31. Vladimir Nabokov – entomologist 32. George Orwell – imperial policeman political pamphleteer 33. Samuel Richardson – printer 34. Antoine de Saint-Exupery – pilot 35. Dorothy L. Sayers – ad writer

36. Walter Scott – attorney 37. Benedict Spinoza – lens grinder 38. Stendhal – Napoleonic dragoon 39. Wallace Stevens – insurance attorney 40. Henry David Thoreau – pencil maker, schoolmaster

41. J.R.R. Tolkien – professor of Anglo-Saxon 42. Mark Twain – steamboat pilot, newspaper reporter 43. Lew Wallace – Civil War general 55. Joseph Wambaugh – police detective 45. William Carlos Williams – pediatrician.

BETTER THAN ONE

George Bernard Shaw possessed a low opinion of literary collaboration. "Two people getting together to write a book," he asserted, "is like three people getting together to have a baby. One of them is superfluous." Agatha Christie added, "I've always believed in writing without a collaborator, because where two people are writing the same book, each believes he gets all the worries and only half the royalties."

But there are times when "two are better than one," as we learn in the Book of Ecclesiastes 4.9.

Identify the dynamic duo of authors of each work.

1. *All the President's Men*
2. *The Communist Manifesto*
3. *The Gilded Age*
4. *Good Omens*
5. *Is Sex Necessary?*

6. *Lyrical Ballads*
7. *The Man Who Came to Dinner*
8. *The President Is Missing*
9. *Tales From Shakespeare*
10. *The Talisman*

11. *The Two Noble Kinsmen*
12. *The Ugly American*
13. *What Price Glory?*

14. *The Wreck of the Golden Mary*
15. *Mutiny On the Bounty*

16. *Peter and the Starcatchers*
17. *The Ship Who Searched*
18. *Traveling With Pomegranates: A Mother-Daughter Story*
19. *Some Sing, Some Cry*
20. *A Shark Out of Water*

Answers

1. Bob Woodward and Carl Bernstein 2. Karl Marx and Friederich Engels 3. Mark Twain and Charles Dudley Warner 4. Neil Gaiman and Terry Pratchett 5. E.B. White and James Thurber

6. William Wordsworth and Samuel Taylor Coleridge 7. George S. Kaufman and Moss Hart 8. Bill Clinton and James Patterson 9. Charles and Mary Lamb 10. Stephen King and Peter Straub

11. John Fletcher and William Shakespeare 12. William J. Lederer and Eugene F. Burdick 13. Maxwell Anderson and Lawrence Stallings 14. Charles Dickens and Wilkie Collins 15. Charles Nordhoff and James Norman Hall

16. Dave Barry and Ridley Pearson 17. Anne McCaffrey and Mercedes Lackey 18. Sue Monk Kidd and Ann Kidd Taylor 19. Ntozake Shange and Ifa Bayleza 20. Mary Jane Latsis and Martha Herissart, writing as Emma Lathen

Literary conjugation has been achieved by a number of husbands and wives, including Will and Ariel Durant *(The Story of Civilization)*, Scott and Helen Nearing *(Living the Good Life)*, and Colette and her husband Willy (the *Claudine* books).

William Butler Yeats claimed that much of his book *Visions* was dictated by his wife, the spiritualist medium Georgie Hyde Lees. (When asked if he had ever seen these spirits, Yeats replied that he hadn't, but he had *smelled* them.)

Writers are attracted to writers. Three of Ernest Hemingway's four wives—Pauline Pfeiffer, Martha Gelhorn, and Mary Welsh—

were accomplished writers, as were all three of Robert Lowell's wives—Jean Stafford, Elizabeth Hardwick, and Caroline Blackwood.

Match these literary wives and literary husbands:

1. Joan Didion	Richard Aldington
2. Hilda Doolittle	Thomas Carlyle
3. Louise Erdrich	Raymond Carver
4. Mary Ann Evans	Michael Dorris
5. Tess Gallagher	John Gregory Dunne
6. Jane Kenyon	Donald Hall
7. Mary McCarthy	Ted Hughes
8. C.L. Moore	Henry Kuttner
9. Sylvia Plath	Nick Laird
10. Zadie Smith	George Henry Lewes
11. Dorothy Thompson	Robert Lowell
12. Jane Welsh	Edmund Wilson

Answers

1. Joan Didion and John Gregory Dunne 2. Hilda Doolittle and Richard Aldington 3. Louise Erdrich and Michael Dorris 4. Mary Ann Evans and George Henry Lewes 5. Tess Gallagher and Raymond Carver 6. Donald Hall and Jane Kenyon

7. Mary McCarthy and Edmund Wilson 8. C.L. Moore and Henry Kuttner 9. Sylvia Plath and Ted Hughes 10. Zadie Smith and Nick Laird 11. Dorothy Thompson and Robert Lowell 12. Jane Welsh and Thomas Carlyle

THE FINAL CHAPTER

When the book of life ends, some men and women deliver closing lines that are recorded for posterity. Not surprisingly, some of the most famous of last words have been uttered by writers, creatively garrulous to the very end.

The Irish playwright Oscar Wilde, always one to turn a clever phrase, called for champagne and quipped, "I am dying as I have lived, beyond my means." Welsh poet Dylan Thomas, who also put the quart before the hearse, slurred, "I've had eighteen straight whiskeys. I think this is a record." And then he died.

German poet Heinrich Heine proclaimed, "God will pardon me. It's his profession." Oliver Goldsmith was more cynical. Dying from a surfeit of James' Fever Powder, a preparation he was expressly forbidden to take, he was asked if his conscience was clear. His last utterance: "No, it is not."

When asked if he had made his peace with God, Henry David Thoreau, just before he died, said, "I was not aware that we had ever quarreled." As she lay dying of cancer, the American expatriate writer Gertrude Stein asked her friend Alice B. Toklas, "What is the answer?" When Ms. Toklas, overcome by grief, could not respond, the writer spoke again: "In that case, what is the question?" When H.G. Wells was on his deathbed, his friends and relatives gathered around and tried to extract some famous last words. The great writer whispered with some impatience, "Can't you see I'm busy dying?"

The journey to "that undiscovered country from whose bourn no traveler returns" can reveal a lot about a person's life.

Identify each author from the description of his or her denouement:

1. This Greek playwright is said to have died of a skull fracture when an eagle dropped a tortoise on his bald head, mistaking it for a rock.

2. This British Lord Chancellor, who wrote *Utopia,* was imprisoned and executed for refusing to sign Henry VIII's oath of supremacy.

3. This American humorist predicted that he would die the same year that Halley's Comet returned (1910), and he did. On the night before that passing, Halley's Comet shone in the skies as it made its closest approach to the earth. Just a year before, he had said to a friend: "I came in with Halley's Comet in 1835. It is coming again next year, and I expect to go out with it. The almighty has said, no doubt, 'Now here go these two unaccountable frauds; they came in together, they must go out together.' Oh! I am looking forward to that." The inscription on his gravestone in Elmira, New York, preserves one of his most famous quotations: "The reports of my death are greatly exaggerated."

4. Although desperately ill, this French actor and dramatist insisted on going on stage so as not to let down the rest of the company. When the play was over, he collapsed and had to be carried home, where he died shortly afterward of a burst blood vessel in his throat.

5. This London man of letters published an annotated edition of *The Plays of Shakespeare.* Years later he was buried in the Poets' Corner of Westminster Abbey at the foot of Shakespeare's statue.

6. This English Romantic poet sailed to Greece to fight in its war for independence from the Ottoman Empire. When he fell ill, the doctors bled him, which weakened his condition and caused sepsis. The poet's death, at thirty-six, created a sensation throughout the literary world.

7. When he was twenty-three, this Romantic poet prophetically wrote:

> When I have fears that I may cease to be
> Before my pen had glean'd my teeming brain,
> Before high piled books in charactery
> Hold like rich garners the full-ripened grain.

A year later he stopped writing because of poor health and died at twenty-five, nevertheless leaving a priceless legacy of luminous poetry. He wished for no name or inscription on his grave, but simply the words "Here lies one whose name was writ in water."

8. This American writer of short stories and poems spent his last days stumbling into Baltimore polling places and casting ballots in return for drinks. While preparing for his wedding, he was found wandering deliriously near a saloon and died, at the age of forty, four days later. A literary rival wrote this obituary: "_____ is dead. He died in Baltimore on Sunday, on October 7. The announcement will startle many, but few will be grieved by it." On his tombstone is engraved, "Nevermore."

9. This American dime novelist often wrote about poor but honest boys, like Ragged Dick and Tattered Tom, who made fortunes through pluck and luck—yet the writer himself died a pauper.

10. This Elizabethan playwright reputedly died on the same day and in the same month that he was born. His death was reported thusly: "_____, Drayton, and Ben Jhonson had a merry meeting, and itt seems drank too hard, for _____ died of a feavour there contracted."

11. After many early successes, this Elizabethan playwright died, when he was but twenty-nine, of stab wounds above the right eye. Some scholars believe that he was killed in a tavern brawl in a dispute over the bill. Others conjecture that he was the victim of political assassination.

12. In 1904, this Russian playwright and short story writer died in Germany right after offering a toast to his wife. His body was

returned to Moscow in a refrigerated railway car in a box marked "Oysters."

13. This Russian novelist died in Astapovo in 1910, trying to escape from his vituperative wife. As he lay on his deathbed, he refused to be converted to the Russian Orthodox Church. "Even in the valley of the shadow of death," he told the priest, "two and two do not make six."

14. This author of such American classics as *The Scarlet Letter* died on a canoe trip in the White Mountains of New Hampshire, accompanied by Franklin Pierce, our fourteenth president. The author had been President Pierce's classmate at Bowdoin College, along with Henry Wadsworth Longfellow.

15. This American poet wrote the poem "I Have a Rendezvous With Death" and then was killed in 1916 during World War I fighting in France with the French Foreign Legion.

16. In 1936, the greatest poet and playwright of modern Spain was arrested in Grenada and executed without trial by Francisco Franco's fascist militia.

17. Dealing with moral issues of universal importance, this French existential novelist and essayist achieved worldwide recognition. In 1960, at the height of his fame, the car he was riding in left the road and smashed into a tree. He died instantly of a skull fracture.

18. This American writer was remembered by this memorial in the lobby of the Baltimore *Sun,* a newspaper with which he was long associated: "If after I depart this vale, you ever remember me and have thought to please my ghost, forgive some sinner and wink your eye at some homely girl."

19. This American writer of fiction committed suicide by firing a shotgun into his head, the same weapon his father had used on himself.

20. During his last two years, this American writer of fiction, when he was on the wagon, drank Coca-Cola by the case instead of the alcohol that had wrecked his life. He died before completing his final novel, *The Last Tycoon.* Only a scattering of people came to

his viewing, prompting Dorothy Parker to say, "Poor son of a bitch," a quotation from his most famous book, *The Great Gatsby*.

21. and 22. These two American confessional poets, who were students together and friends after, both committed suicide. The first died at the age of thirty after placing her head in an oven and turning on the gas, the second at the age of forty-six after gassing herself in her garage.

23. In 1969 at the age of thirty-two, this American writer committed suicide in despair over his inability to find a publisher for *A Confederacy of Dunces*. It was published posthumously eleven years after.

24. This Russian author died of "an artery burst in the lungs," just as he had actually dictated in a third-person account of his own death. More than a hundred thousand people spontaneously lined the streets at his funeral, the largest funeral procession for any writer in history.

25. This Hungarian/British political writer often expressed his belief in the right to euthanasia. Late in life, he suffered from Parkinson's disease, and he and his wife committed suicide.

Answers

1. Aeschylus 2. Thomas More 3. Mark Twain 4. Moliere 5. Samuel Johnson

6. Lord Byron 7. John Keats 8. Edgar Allan Poe 9. Horatio Alger 10. William Shakespeare

11. Christopher Marlowe 12. Anton Chekhov 13. Leo Tolstoy 14. Nathaniel Hawthorne 15. Alan Seeger

16. Frederico Garcia Lorca 17. Albert Camus 18. H.L. Mencken 19. Ernest Hemingway 20. F. Scott Fitzgerald

21. Sylvia Plath 22. Anne Sexton 23. John Kennedy Toole 24. Fyodor Dostoevsky 25. Arthur Koestler

WORKS

TRY THESE FOR OPENERS

"Write dramatic, button-holing leads to your stories," James Thurber's editor commanded during his early days as a newspaper reporter. In response, Thurber turned in a murder story that began, "Dead. That's what the man was when they found him with a knife in his back at 4 p.m. in front of Riley's Saloon at the corner of 52nd and 12th Streets."

Isaac Asimov told the story of an author whose agent advised him that his books weren't selling because there wasn't enough sex in them.

"What are you talking about?" objected the author. "Look, right here on the first page, the courtesan dashes out of the room stark naked and runs out into the street with the hero pursuing her just as naked and in an explicitly described state of sexual arousal!"

"Yes, yes," granted the agent, "but look how *far down* on the first page!"

Some famous first words are so effective and well known that readers can look at them and identify the literary works that they lead off.

Identify the novel or short story started by each passage.

1. Dorothy lived in the midst of the great Kansas prairies, with Uncle Henry, who was a farmer, and Auntie Em, who was the farmer's wife. – *L. Frank Baum*

2. All children, except one, grow up. – *James M. Barrie*

3. You don't know about me without you have read a book called *The Adventures of Tom Sawyer*, but that ain't no matter. – *Mark Twain*

4. Alice was beginning to get very tired of sitting by her sister on the bank, and of having nothing to do. – *Lewis Carroll*

5. Call me Ishmael. – *Herman Melville*

6. It is a truth universally acknowledged that a single man in possession of a good fortune must be in want of a wife. – *Jane Austen*

7. It was love at first sight. – *Joseph Heller*

8. What can you say about a twenty-five-year-old girl who died? – *Erich Segal*

9. Mr. and Mrs. Dursley, of number four Privet Drive, were proud to say that they were perfectly normal, thank you very much. They were the last people you'd expect to be involved in anything strange or mysterious, because they just didn't hold with such nonsense. – *J.K. Rowling*

10. It was the best of times, it was the worst of times, it was the age of wisdom, it was the age of foolishness, it was the epoch of belief, it was the epoch of incredulity, it was the season of Light, it was the season of Darkness, it was the spring of hope, it was the winter of despair, we had everything before us, we had nothing before us, we were all going direct to Heaven, we were all going direct the other way. – *Charles Dickens*

11. It was Wang Lung's marriage day. – *Pearl Buck*

12. "Christmas won't be Christmas without any presents," grumbled Jo, lying on the rug. – *Louisa May Alcott*

13. To the red country and part of the gray country of Oklahoma, the last rains came gently, and they did not cut the scarred earth. – *John Steinbeck*

14. One of the very first bullets comes in through the open window above the toilet where Luca is standing. – *Jeanine Cummins*

15. James Bond, with two double bourbons inside him, sat back in the final departure lounge of Miami Airport and thought about life and death. – *Ian Fleming*

16. Renowned curator Jacques Saunière staggered through the vaulted archway of the museum's Grand Gallery. – *Dan Brown*

17. As Gregor Samsa awoke one morning from uneasy dreams, he found himself transformed into a giant insect. – *Franz Kafka*

18. Buck did not read the newspapers or he would have known that trouble was brewing, not alone for himself, but for every tide-water dog, strong of muscle and with warm, long hair, from Puget Sound to San Diego. – *Jack London*

19. When he was nearly thirteen, my brother Jem got his arm badly broken at the elbow. – *Harper Lee*

20. He was an old man who fished alone in a skiff in the Gulf Stream and he had gone eighty-four days now without taking a fish. – *Ernest Hemingway*

21. When Mrs. Frederick C. Little's second son arrived, everybody noticed that he was not much bigger than a mouse. – *E.B. White*

22. A squat, grey building of only thirty-four stories. Over the main entrance the words, CENTRAL LONDON HATCHERY AND CONDITIONING CENTRE, and, in a shield, the World State's motto, COMMUNITY, IDENTITY, STABILITY. – *Aldous Huxley*

23. It was a bright cold day in April, and the clocks were striking thirteen. – *George Orwell*

24. On the morning of August 8, 1965, Robert Kincaid locked the door to his small two-room apartment on the third floor of a rambling house in Bellingham, Washington. – *Robert James Waller*

25. Not so long ago, a monster came to the small town of Castle Rock, Maine. – *Stephen King*

26. I first met Dean not long after my wife and I split up. I had just gotten over a serious illness that I won't bother to talk about, except that it had something to do with the miserably weary split-up and my feeling that everything was dead. With the coming of Dean Moriarty began the part of my life you could call my life on the road. – *Jack Kerouac*

27. We were somewhere around Barstow, on the edge of the desert, when the drugs began to take hold. – *Hunter S. Thompson*

28. Nothing to be done. – *Samuel Beckett*

29. It was a dark and stormy night. – *Edward Bulwer – Lytton/ Madeline L'Engle*

30. Brrrrrrriiiiiiiiiiiiiiiiiiiinng! – *Richard Wright*

31. They're out there. Black boys in white suits up before me to commit sex acts in the hall and get it mopped up before I catch them. – *Ken Kesey*

32. The boy with fair hair lowered himself down the last few feet of rock and began to pick his way toward the lagoon. – *William Golding*

33. A throng of bearded men, in sad-colored garments and gray, steeple-crowned hats, intermixed with women, some wearing hoods, and others bareheaded, was assembled in front of a wooden edifice, the door of which was heavily timbered with oak, and studded with iron spikes. – *Nathaniel Hawthorne*

34. All this happened, more or less. – *Kurt Vonnegut*

35. In the week before their departure to Arrakis, when all the final scurrying about had reached a nearly unbearable frenzy, an old crone came to visit the mother of the boy, Paul." – *Frank Herbert*

36. Amerigo Bonasera sat in New York Criminal Court Number 3 and waited for justice; vengeance on the men who had so cruelly hurt his daughter, who had tried to dishonor her. – *Mario Puzo*

37. It was morning, and the new sun sparkled gold across the ripples of a gentle sea. A mile from shore, a fishing boat chummed the water, and the word for Breakfast Flock flashed through the air, till a crowd of a thousand seagulls came to dodge and fight for bits of food. – *Richard Bach*

38. There were 117 psychoanalysts on the Pan Am flight to Vienna and I'd been treated by at least six of them. – *Erica Jong*

39. If you really want to hear about it, the first thing you'll probably want to know is where I was born, and what my lousy childhood was like, and how my parents were occupied and all before they had

me, and all that David Copperfield kind of crap, but I don't feel like going into it, if you want to know the truth. – *J.D. Salinger*

40. Happy families are all alike; every unhappy family is unhappy in its own way. – *Leo Tolstoy*

41. We slept in what had been the gymnasium. – *Margaret Atwood*

42. 124 was spiteful. Full of baby venom. – *Toni Morrison*

43. Somewhere in La Mancha, in a place whose name I do not care to remember, a gentleman lived not long ago, one of those who has a lance and ancient shield on a shelf and keeps a skinny nag and a greyhound for racing. – *Miguel de Cervantes*

44. Ships at a distance have every man's wish on board. – *Zora Neale Hurston*

45. In my younger and more vulnerable years, my father gave me some advice that I have been turning over in my head ever since. – *F. Scott Fitzgerald*

46. Scarlett O'Hara was not beautiful, but men seldom realized it when caught by her charm as the Tarleton twins were. – *Margaret Mitchell*

47. He was born with a gift of laughter and a sense that the world was mad. – *Raphael Sabatini*

48. It was a queer, sultry summer, the summer they electrocuted the Rosenbergs, and I didn't know what I was doing in New York. – *Sylvia Plath*

49. I am an invisible man. – *Ralph Ellison*

50. You better not never tell nobody but God. – *Alice Walker*

51. Far out in the uncharted backwaters of the unfashionable end of the western spiral arm of the Galaxy lies a small, unregarded yellow sun. – *Douglas Adams*

52. Once there were four children whose names were Peter, Susan, Edmund, and Lucy. This story is something that happened to them when they were sent away from London during the war – *C.S. Lewis*

53. There was no possibility of taking a walk that day. – *Charlotte Brontë*

54. My name was Salmon, like the fish; first name, Susie. I was fourteen when I was murdered on December 6, 1973. – *Alice Seebold*

55. It was a pleasure to burn. – *Ray Bradbury*

56. There are some men who enter a woman's life and screw it up forever. Joseph Morelli did this to me—not forever, but periodically. – *Janet Evanovich*

57. Through the fence, between the curling flower spaces, I could see them hitting. – *William Faulkner*

58. This is my favorite book in all the world, though I have never read it. – *William Goldman*

59. I am an American, Chicago born—Chicago, that somber city—and go at things as I have taught myself, free-style, and will make the record in my own way; first to knock, sometimes an innocent knock, sometimes a not so innocent. – *Saul Bellow*

60. Once upon a time and a very good time it was there was a moocow coming down along the road and this moocow that was coming down along the road met a nicens little boy named baby tuckoo. – *James Joyce*

Answers

1. *The Wonderful Wizard of Oz* 2. *Peter Pan* 3. *The Adventures of Huckleberry Finn* 4. *Alice's Adventures in Wonderland* 5. *Moby-Dick*

6. *Pride and Prejudice* 7. *Catch-22* 8. *Love Story* 9. *Harry Potter and the Philosopher's Stone* 10. *A Tale of Two Cities*

11. *The Good Earth* 12. *Little Women* 13. *The Grapes of Wrath* 14. *American Dirt* 15. *Goldfinger*

16. *The Da Vinci Code* 17. "The Metamorphosis" 18. *The Call of the Wild* 19. *To Kill a Mockingbird* 20. *The Old Man and the Sea*

21. *Stuart Little* 22. *Brave New World* 23. *Nineteen Eighty-Four* 24. *The Bridges of Madison County* 25. *Cujo*

26. *On the Road* 27. *Fear and Loathing in Las Vegas* 28. *Waiting For Godot* 29. *Paul Clifford/A Wrinkle in Time* 30. *Native Son*

31. *One Flew Over the Cuckoo's Nest* 32. *Lord of the Flies* 33. *The Scarlet Letter* 34. *Slaughterhouse-Five* 35. *Dune*

36. *The Godfather* 37. *Jonathan Livingston Seagull* 38. *Fear Of Flying* 39. *The Catcher in the Rye* 40. *Anna Karenina*

41. *The Handmaid's Tale* 42. *Beloved* 43. *Don Quixote* 44. *Their Eyes Were Watching God* 45. *The Great Gatsby*

46. *Gone With the Wind* 47. *Scaramouche* 48. *The Bell Jar* 49. *Invisible Man* 50. *The Color Purple*

51. *A Hitchhiker's Guide To the Galaxy* 52. *The Lion, the Witch, and the Wardrobe* 53. *Jane Eyre* 54. *The Lovely Bones* 55. *Fahrenheit 451*

56. *One for the Money* 57. *The Sound and the Fury* 58. *The Princess Bride* 59. *The Adventures of Augie March* 60. *A Portrait of the Artist As a Young Man*

PERFECT MATCHES

Match each real or imaginary person in the left-hand column with his or her perfect literary title in the right-hand column. Let's start with a cast of imaginary people, such as Apollo, *The Sun Also Rises;* King Midas, *Goldfinger;* Barney the Dinosaur, *The Color Purple;* and Hansel and Gretel, *A Walk In the Woods.*

1. Captain Ahab	*Arms and the Man*
2. Ben-Hur	*The Big Sleep*
3. Bugs Bunny	*Chariots of Fire*
4. Chicken Little	*A Farewell to Arms*
5. Count Dracula	*Fences*
6. Lemuel Gulliver	*For Whom the Bell Tolls*
7. Lady Macbeth	*Giant*
8. Popeye	*The Jungle*
9. Hester Prynne	*The King Must Die*
10. Quasimodo	*Magnificent Obsession*
11. Tom Sawyer	*Marley and Me*
12. Ebenezer Scrooge	*Rabbit Run*
13. Tarzan	*The Red Badge of Courage*
14. Rip Van Winkle	*Skyfall*
15. Venus de Milo	*White Fang*

Answers

1. *Magnificent Obsession* 2. *Chariots of Fire* 3. *Rabbit Run* 4. *Skyfall* 5. *White Fang*

6. *Giant* 7. *The King Must Die* 8. *Arms and the Man* 9. *The Red Badge of Courage* 10. *For Whom the Bell Tolls*

11. *Fences* 12. *Marley and Me* 13. *The Jungle* 14. *The Big Sleep* 15. *A Farewell to Arms*

Now match each real-life person with his or her perfect book title. Examples: Yogi Berra, *Catcher in the Rye,* and Amelia Earhart, *Gone Girl.*

1. John and Priscilla Alden	*The Birds*
2. Louis Armstrong	*Black Beauty*
3. Neil Armstrong	*The Bluest Eye*
4. Benedict Arnold	*The Boys in the Band*
5. John Jay Audubon	*Brave New World*
6. The Beatles	*The Cherry Orchard*
7. Jeff Bezos	*Come Blow Your Horn*
8. Camilla Parker Bowles	*Crime and Punishment*
9. Al Capone	*Deliverance*
10. Christopher Columbus	*An Enemy of the People*
11. Thomas Crapper	*Game of Thrones*
12. Euclid	*The Good Earth*
13. Anthony Fauci	*The Grapes of Wrath*
14. W.C. Fields	*Heart Of Darkness*
15. Benjamin Franklin	*The Hitchhiker's Guide to the Galaxy*
16. Jane Goodall	*The Iceman Cometh*
17. Wayne Gretzky	*Jaws*
18. Harry and Meghan	*The Kite Runner*
19. Adolph Hitler	*Life of Pi*
20. Jay Leno	*Lord of the Flies*
21. Bruno Mars	*Love Story*

and Venus Williams	*Men Are From Mars,*
22. Willie Mays	*Women Are From Venus*
23. Mona Lisa	*Moonwalk*
24. Moses	*The Once and Future King*
25. John Muir	*The Pilgrim's Progress*
26. Elvis Presley	*The Plague*
27. Frank Sinatra	*Planet of the Apes*
28. Neil deGrasse Tyson	*The Portrait of a Lady*
29. George Washington	*Travels With Charley*
30. Vanessa Williams	*Up From Slavery*

Answers

1. *Pilgrim's Progress* 2. *Come Blow Your Horn* 3. *Moonwalk* 4. *An Enemy of the People* 5. *The Birds*

6. *The Boys in the Band* 7. *Deliverance* 8. *Travels With Charlie* 9. *Crime and Punishment* 10. *Brave New World*

11. *Game Of Thrones* 12. *Life Of Pi* 13. *The Plague* 14. *The Grapes of Wrath* 15. *The Kite Runner*

16. *Planet of the Apes* 17. *The Iceman Cometh* 18. *Love Story* 19. *Heart of Darkness* 20. *Jaws*

21. *Men Are From Mars, Women Are From Venus* 22. *Lord of the Flies* 23. *The Portrait of a Lady* 24. *Up From Slavery* 25. *The Good Earth*

26. *The Once and Future King* 27. *The Bluest Eye* 28. *The Hitchhiker's Guide to the Galaxy* 29. *The Cherry Orchard* 30. *Black Beauty*

Unreal Estate

He wrote under the pseudonyms Schuyler Stanton, Floyd Akers, and Edith Van Dyne, but he is best known as L. Frank Baum. In 1900, he sat down to write a children's book about a girl named Dorothy, who was swept away to a fantastic land inhabited by munchkins and witches and a scarecrow, a tin man, and a lion.

The fairy tale began as a bedtime story for Baum's children and their friends and soon spilled over into several evening sessions. During one of the tellings, Baum was asked the name of the strange place to which Dorothy was swept away. Glancing about the room, Baum's eyes fell upon the drawers of a filing cabinet labeled "A-N" and "O-Z."

Noting that the letters on the second label spelled out the *ahs* uttered by his rapt listeners, Baum named his fantastic land Oz. Ever since, *The Wonderful Wizard of Oz* has lived in the hearts of children—and grown-ups.

For many lovers of literature, places that exist only between the covers of books are as vivid as places that actually exist. If you are one of those people for whom Oz is as real as Oslo, Camelot is as real as Camden, and Wonderland is as real as Disneyland, this quiz is for you.

Match each imaginary locale listed in the left-hand column with the name of its creator listed in the right-hand column:

1. Baskerville Hall	Sherwood Anderson
2. Belle Reeve	Piers Anthony
3. Bleak House	Aristophanes
4. Brideshead	Jane Austen
5. Cloud Cuckoo Land	James M. Barrie
6. Darkover	L. Frank Baum
7. DuneMarion	Zimmer Bradley
8. East Egg	Charlotte Brontë
9. Egdon Heath	Emily Brontë
10. The Emerald City	John Bunyan
11. The Forest of Arden	Lewis Carroll
12. Gopher Prairie	Miguel de Cervantes
13. Hogwarts School	Samuel Taylor Coleridge
14. La Mancha	Charles Dickens
15. Land of the Lotus-Eaters	Arthur Conan Doyle
16. Lilliput	George Eliot
17. Looking-Glass House	William Faulkner
18. Lowood	F. Scott Fitzgerald
19. Middle Earth	Kenneth Grahame
20. Middlemarch	Thomas Hardy
21. Narnia	Frank Herbert
22. Never-Never-Land	James Hilton
23. Northanger Abbey	Homer
24. Oceania	Stephen King
25. Pandemonium	C.S. Lewis
26. Pencey Prep	Sinclair Lewis
27. Pooh Corner	A.A. Milne
28. The Republic	John Milton
29. Salem's Lot	Thomas More
30. Shangri-La	George Orwell
31. The Slough of Despond	Plato
32. Starkville	J.K. Rowling
33. Toad Hall	J.D. Salinger

34. Utopia	Walter Scott
35. Waverley Hall	William Shakespeare
36. Winesburg	Jonathan Swift
37. Wuthering Heights	J.R.R. Tolkien
38. Xanadu	Evelyn Waugh
39. Xanth	Edith Wharton
40. Yoknapatawpha County	Tennessee Williams

Answers

1. Arthur Conan Doyle 2. Tennessee Williams 3. Charles Dickens 4. Evelyn Waugh 5. Aristophanes

6. Marion Zimmer Bradley 7. Frank Herbert 8. F. Scott Fitzgerald 9. Thomas Hardy 10. L. Frank Baum

11. William Shakespeare 12. Sinclair Lewis 13. J.K. Rowling 14. Miguel de Cervantes 15. Homer

16. Jonathan Swift 17. Lewis Carroll 18. Charlotte Brontë 19. J.R.R. Tolkien 20. George Eliot

21. C.S. Lewis 22. James M. Barrie 23. Jane Austen 24. George Orwell 25. John Milton

26. J.D. Salinger 27. A.A. Milne 28. Plato 29. Stephen King 30. James Hilton

31. John Bunyan 32. Edith Wharton 33. Kenneth Grahame 34. Thomas More 35. Walter Scott

36. Sherwood Anderson 37. Emily Brontë 38. Samuel Taylor Coleridge 39. Piers Anthony 40. William Faulkner

SUPER SLEUTHS

Arthur Conan Doyle wanted to give his fictional detective an out-landish first name and thought seriously about Sherrinford. Ultimately, the doctor turned author settled on the Christian name Sherlock, after a Yorkshire bowler named Mordecai Sherlock, against whom he had played cricket.

After seriously considering the last name of Hope, suggested by a whaling ship named the *Hope,* Doyle chose that of a much-admired American writer of the time, Oliver Wendell Holmes. A distinguished, brilliant, and multitalented pioneer in medicine and criminal psychology, Oliver Wendell was the perfect prototype for Doyle's consulting detective. That's why the world's most famous fictional sleuth isn't known as Sherrinford Hope.

Dashiell Hammett gave his most famous creation his own first name, which was Sam, as in Samuel Dashiell Hammett. Now you know why the classic hard-boiled detective in *The Maltese Falcon* came close to being named Dash Spade.

The word *sleuth* is a clipping of *sleuthhound,* the Scottish bloodhound noted for its dogged pursuit of game, suspects, or fugitive.

Match each author in the left-hand column with his or her sleuth to the right.

1. Margery Allingham	Roderick Alleyn
2. Martin Amis	Lew Archer
3. Nevada Barr	Harry Bosch
4. Edmund Clerihew Bentley	Father Brown
5. Earl Derr Biggers	Brother Cadfael
6. Jim Butcher	Albert Campion
7. John Dickson Carr	Steve Carella
8. Raymond Chandler	Charlie Chan
9. Leslie Charteris	Nick and Nora Charles
10. G.K. Chesterton	Jim Chee
11. Lee Child	Sergeant Cribb
12. Agatha Christie	Harry Dresden
13. Ann Cleaves	Nancy Drew
14. Michael Connolly	C. Auguste Dupin
15. Patricia Cornwell	Dr. Gideon Fell
16. Edmund Crispin	Gervase Fen
17. Janet Evanovich	Alan Grant
18. Antonia Fraser	Cordelia Gray
19. Emile Gaboriau	Mike Hammer
20. Erle Stanley Gardner	Mike Hoolihan
21. Sue Grafton	Richard Jury
22. Martha Grimes	Monsieur Lecoq
23. Dashiell Hammett	Inspector Maigret
24. Tony Hillerman	Philip Marlowe
25. P.D. James	Jane Marple
26. Carolyn Keene	Perry Mason
27. Harry Kemelman	Travis McGee
28. Peter Lovesey	Kinsey Millhone
29. John D. MacDonald	Amelia Peabody
30. Ross MacDonald	Anna Pigeon
31. Ngaio Marsh	Stephanie Plum
32. Ed McBain	Peter Porteous
33. Walter Mosley	Easy Rawlins

34. Sara Paretsky	Jack Reacher
35. Ellis Peters	Arkady Renko
36. Elizabeth Peters	The Saint (Simon Templar)
37. Edgar Allan Poe	Kay Scarpetta
38. Ruth Rendell	Jemima Shore
39. Dorothy L. Sayers	Rabbi David Small
40. Georges Simenon	Philip Trent
41. Martin Cruz Smith	Philo Vance
42. Mickey Spillane	V. I. Warshawski
43. Rex Stout	Reginald Wexford
44. Josephine Tey	Lord Peter Wimsey
45. S.S. Van Dine	Nero Wolfe

Answers

1. Margery Allingham – Albert Campion 2. Martin Amis – Mike Hoolihan 3. Nevada Barr – Anna Pigeon 4. Edmund Clerihew Bentley – Philip Trent 5. Earl Derr Biggers – Charlie Chan

6. Jim Butcher – Harry Dresden 7. John Dickson Carr – Dr. Gideon Fell 8. Raymond Chandler – Philip Marlowe 9. Lee Child – Jack Reacher 10. Leslie Charteris – The Saint (Simon Templar)

11. G.K. Chesterton – Father Brown 12. Agatha Christie – Jane Marple 13. Ann Cleeves – Peter Porteous 14. Mike Connelly – Harry Bosch 15. Patricia Cornwell – Kay Scarpetta

16. Edmund Crispin – Gervase Fen 17. Janet Evanovich – Stephanie Plum 18. Antonia Fraser – Jemima Shore 19. Emile Gaboriau – Monsieur Lecoq 20. Erle Stanley Gardner – Perry Mason

21. Sue Grafton – Kinsey Millhone 22. Martha Grimes – Richard Jury 23. Dashiell Hammett – Nick and Nora Charles 24. Tony Hillerman – Jim Chee 25. P.D. James – Cordelia Gray

26. Carolyn Keene – Nancy Drew 27. Harry Kemelman – Rabbi David Small 28. Peter Lovesey – Sergeant Cribb 29. John D. MacDonald – Travis McGee 30. Ross MacDonald – Lew Archer

31. Ngaio Marsh – Roderick Alleyn 32. Ed McBain – Steve Carella 33. Walter Mosley – Easy Rawlins 34. Sara Paretsky – V.I. Warshawski 35. Elizabeth Peters – Amelia Peabody

36. Ellis Peters – Brother Cadfael 37. Edgar Allan Poe – C. Auguste Dupin 38. Ruth Rendell – Reginald Wexford 39. Martin Cruz Smith – Arkady Renko 40. Dorothy L. Sayers – Lord Peter Wimsey

41. Rex Stout – Nero Wolfe 42. Josephine Tey – Alan Grant 43. Georges Simenon – Inspector Maigret 44. Mickey Spillane – Mike Hammer 45. S.S. Van Dine – Philo Vance

WAR GAME

"Like me to write you a little essay on The Importance of Subject?" wrote Ernest Hemingway to F. Scott Fitzgerald. "Well the reason you are so sore you missed the war is because war is the best subject of all. It groups the maximum of material and speeds up the action and brings out all sorts of stuff that normally you have to wait a lifetime to get."

Fitzgerald was commissioned a second lieutenant in the U.S. Army Infantry in 1917, but never served abroad, while Hemingway was an American Red Cross ambulance driver in Italy during World War I.

A number of other writers have had firsthand experience with that "best subject of all." Ambrose Bierce enlisted twice in the Ninth Indiana Infantry and fought in a great many Civil War skirmishes and battles, including Philippi and Shiloh. In 1867, he was promoted to major in recognition of his heroism and distinguished service and later wrote some twenty-five short stories about his war experiences, among them "An Occurrence at Owl Creek Bridge" and "Chickamauga." In 1862 and 1863 Walt Whitman served as a copyist in the army paymaster's office and spent his afternoons nursing the wounded in nearby military hospitals. He recorded his experiences and emotions in *Drum Taps*.

The best-known novel about the American Civil War is Stephen Crane's *The Red Badge of Courage*. So vividly realistic is Crane's account of Henry Fleming's discoveries of war and his own manhood that many readers believe the author must have fought in the war. In fact, a number of Civil War veterans swore up and down that

Crane had fought next to them on the battlefield. But Crane never participated in the War Between the States, one convincing proof being the fact that he was not born until 1871.

The following works are grouped chronologically according to the wars they describe. Identify the author of each work:

1. The Trojan War: *Iliad, Troilus and Criseyde, Troilus and Cressida*
2. Peloponnesian Wars: *Lysistrata, The Last of the Wine*
3. The Crusades: *The Talisman*
4. Hundred Years' War: *Henry V*
5. French and Indian War: *The Last of the Mohicans, Montcalm and Wolfe*

6. American Revolutionary War: *April Morning, Johnny Tremaine, Drums Along the Mohawk, The Spy*
7. French Revolution: *A Tale of Two Cities*
8. Napoleonic Wars: *War and Peace*
9. War of 1812: "Old Ironsides," *Captain Caution*
10. Crimean War: "The Charge of the Light Brigade"

11. American Civil War: *John Brown's Body, Andersonville, Gone with the Wind*
12. World War I: *A Farewell to Arms,* "Dulce Et Decorum Est" *All Quiet on the Western Front, The Enormous Room,*
13. Russian Revolution: *Ten Days That Shook the World*
14. Spanish Civil War: *For Whom the Bell Tolls*
15. World War II: *Catch-22, A Bell for Adano, The Naked and the Dead, Slaughterhouse-Five*

16. Korean War: *The Bridges at Toko-Ri*
17. Viet Nam War: *The Green Berets, Dog Soldiers, Going After Cacciato*
18. Gulf War: *Bravo Two Zero, The One That Got Away, Jarhead*
19. Iraq War: *Lost in America*
20. Afghanistan War: *Seal Team 666*

Answers

1. Homer, Geoffrey Chaucer, William Shakespeare 2. Aristophanes, Mary Renault 3. Walter Scott 4. William Shakespeare 5. James Fenimore Cooper, Francis Parkman

6. Howard Fast, Esther Forbes, Walter D. Edmonds, James Fenimore Cooper 7. Charles Dickens 8. Leo Tolstoy 9. Oliver Wendell Holmes, Kenneth Roberts 10. Alfred, Lord Tennyson

11. Stephen Vincent Benét, MacKinlay Kantor, Margaret Mitchell 12. Ernest Hemingway, Wilfred Owen, Erich Maria Remarque, e.e. cummings, 13. John Reed 14. Ernest Hemingway 15. Joseph Heller, John Hersey, Norman Mailer, Kurt Vonnegut

16. James Michener 17. Robin Moore, Robert Stone, Tim O'Brien 18. Andy McNab, Chris Ryan, Anthony Swofford 19. Colby Buzzell 20. Weston Ochse

Notable, Quotable Poetry

"There's no money in poetry," quoth the poet laureate Robert Graves, "but there's also no poetry in money." While it is true that rhyme doesn't pay, poets gain a foothold on eternity through their poems, which for some people is even better than money. What follows are some of the most memorable and enduring lines in the mighty line of English poetry.

Identify the sources of the following quotations by title and author:

1. Whan that Aprill with his shoures soote
   The droghte of March hath perced to the roote

2. Shall I compare thee to a summer's day?
   Thou art more lovely and more temperate.

3. Death be not proud

4. 'Twas brillig, and the slithy toves
   Did gyre and gimble in the wabe:
   All mimsy were the borogoves,
   And the mome raths outgrabe.

5. Drink to me only with thine eyes,
   And I will pledge with mine

6. Listen, my children, and you will hear
   Of the midnight ride of Paul Revere.
   On the eighteenth of April in seventy-five;
   Hardly a man is now alive
   Who remembers that famous day and year.

7. The outlook wasn't brilliant
   For the Mudville nine that day.
   The score stood four to two,
   With but one inning left to play.

8. Gather ye rosebuds while ye may.
   Old Time is still a-flying.

9. Once upon a midnight dreary,
   While I pondered, weak and weary,
   Over many a quaint and curious
   Volume of forgotten lore,—

10. But at my back I always hear
    Time's wingèd chariot hurrying near

11. They also serve who only stand and wait.

12. Know then thyself, presume not God to scan;
    The proper study of mankind is man.

13. Should auld acquaintance be forgot,
    And never brought to min'?
    Should auld acquaintance be forgot,
    And days o' auld lang syne?

14. Tiger! Tiger! Burning bright
    In the forest of the night.
    What immortal hand or eye
    Could frame they fearful symmetry?

15. Water, water everywhere,
    Nor any drop to drink.

16. Hope springs eternal in the human breast.

17. A thing of beauty is a joy forever.

18. If winter comes, can spring be far behind?

19. Beauty is truth, truth beauty.

20. A Book of Verses underneath the Bough,
    A Jug of Wine, a Loaf of Bread—and Thou

21. God's in his heaven—
    All's right with the world.

22. How do I love thee? Let me count the ways.

23. A little learning is a dangerous thing.

24. Do not go gentle into that good night...
    Rage, rage against the dying of the light.

25. By the shores of Gitche Gumee
    By the shining Big-Sea-Water

26. Behind him lay the gray Azores,
    Behind the Gates of Hercules;
    Before him not the ghost of shores,
    Before him only shoreless seas.

27. O Captain! My Captain!
    Our fearful trip is done,
    The ship has weathered every rack,
    The prize we sought is won.

28. Because I could not stop for Death,
    He kindly stopped for me—

29. This is the way the world ends
    Not with a bang but a whimper.

30. The fog comes
    On little cat feet.

31. The woods are lovely, dark and deep,
    But I have promises to keep.

32. Out of the night that covers me,
    Black as the Pit from pole to pole,
    I thank whatever gods may be
    For my unconquerable soul.

33. I must go down to the seas again,
    To the lonely sea and the sky.
    And all I ask is a tall ship
    And a star to steer her by.

34. Theirs not to make reply,
    Theirs not to reason why,
    Theirs but to do and die;
    Into the valley of Death
    Rode the six hundred.

35. 'Twas the night before Christmas,
    When all through the house
    Not a creature was stirring,
    Not even a mouse.

Answers

1. Prologue to *The Canterbury Tales,* Geoffrey Chaucer 2. Sonnet XVIII, William Shakespeare 3. "Death Be Not Proud," John Donne 4. "Jabberwocky," Lewis Carroll 5. "Song to Celia," Ben Jonson

6. "Paul Revere's Ride," Henry Wadsworth Longfellow 7. "Casey at the Bat," Ernest Lawrence Thayer 8. "To the Virgins, to Make Much of Time," Robert Herrick 9. "The Raven," Edgar Allan Poe 10. "To His Coy Mistress," Andrew Marvell

11. "On His Blindness," John Milton 12. "An Essay on Man," Alexander Pope 13. "Auld Lang Syne," Robert Burns 14. "The Tiger," William Blake 15. "The Rime of the Ancient Mariner," Samuel Taylor Coleridge

16. "Essay on Man," Alexander Pope 17. *Endymion,* John Keats 18. "Ode to the West Wind," Percy Bysshe Shelley 19. "Ode on a Grecian Urn," John Keats 20. *The Rubaiyat of Omar Khayyam,* Edward Fitzgerald

21. *Pippa Passes,* Robert Browning 22. Sonnet 43, in *Sonnets from the Portuguese,* Elizabeth Barrett Browning 23. "Essay on Criticism," Alexander Pope 24. "Do Not Go Gentle Into That Good Night," Dylan Thomas 25. "The Song of Hiawatha," Henry Wadsworth Longfellow

26. "Columbus," Joaquin Miller 27. "O Captain! My Captain!," Walt Whitman 28. "Because I could not stop for Death," Emily Dickinson 29. "The Hollow Men," T.S. Eliot 30. "Fog," Carl Sandburg

31. "Stopping by Woods on a Snowy Evening," Robert Frost 32. "Invictus," William Ernest Henley 33. "Sea-Fever," John Masefield 34. "The Charge of the Light Brigade," Alfred, Lord Tennyson 35. "A Visit From St. Nicholas," also known as "The Night Before Christmas," Clement Clarke Moore

BORN AT THE TIP OF A PEN

When people misuse words in an illiterate but humorous manner, we call the result a *malapropism*. The word echoes the name of Mrs. Malaprop (from the French *mal à propos,* "not appropriate"), a character who first strode the stage in 1775 in Richard Sheridan's comedy *The Rivals.* Mrs. Malaprop was an "old weather-beaten she dragon" who took special pride in her use of the King's English but who unfailingly mangled big words all the same: "Sure, if I reprehend anything in this world it is the use of my oracular tongue, and a nice derangement of epitaphs!" She meant, of course, that if she comprehended anything, it was a nice arrangement of epithets.

A number of words have been literally and literarily born at the tip of a pen, for our language bestows a special kind of life upon people and places that have existed only in books. Fictional creations though they may be, many of these literary creations have assumed a vitality and longevity that pulse just as powerfully as their flesh-and-blood counterparts. The words that derive from these imaginary names can achieve such wide application that they are no longer written with capital letters.

Using the following descriptions, identify the common words that have sprung from the fertile imaginations of our novelists, playwrights, and poets. Also identify the original names of the characters or works whence they spring.

1. The hero of a novel by Miguel de Cervantes engaged himself in endless knightly quests, rescuing damsels he deemed to be in distress and fighting monsters by tilting against windmills. An adjective formed from his name now describes people who are idealistic and chivalrous to an extravagant degree.

2. The name of a blustering giant in Edmund Spenser's Renaissance epic, *The Faerie Queene,* has become a word for a loud-mouthed boaster who is notably short on performance.

3. Another big-talking giant lumbers through the pages of a novel by François Rabelais. This giant king was so huge that it took 17,913 cows to provide him with milk and eleven hundred hides to make him a pair of shoes. Today an adjective form of his name denotes anything of a colossal scale.

4. In 1516, Thomas More wrote a book about an ideal state. As a name for both the novel and the place, More coined a name from the Greek word parts *ou,* "no," *topos,* "place," and – *ia,* "state of being." The resulting word has come to designate any ideal society.

5. The imagination of Charles Dickens teemed with colorful characters who so embodied particular traits in human nature that their names have come to stand for those qualities. Thus, a fawning toady is often called a *Uriah Heep* and a tyrannical teacher a *Gradgrind. Micawberish* has become a synonym for "habitually hopeful" and *Pecksniffery* a noun for religious hypocrisy. These name words have retained their capital letters, but one that is rapidly evolving into lower case began life as a character in *A Christmas Carol.* Even though old Ebenezer's heart turned from stone to gold at the end of the story, we still use his name to describe a mean and miserly person.

Answers

1. Don Quixote-quixotic 2. Braggadocio-braggadocio 3. Gargantua-gargantuan 4. *Utopia*–utopia, utopian 5. Scrooge-scrooge

English is a cheerfully hospitable language that welcomes into its realm words near and far, ancient and modern, and of high and low station. It's no surprise, then, that folkloric characters from cartoons, comic strips, and comic books have leapt from the newspapers and screen into our everyday speech and writing.

In 1928, Walt Disney gave the world a Mickey—an all-American rodent who performed heroic deeds and squeaked his undying love for Minnie. Soon after World War II, international markets were flooded with wristwatches bearing Mickey's likeness. Because these watches were generally cheap affairs subject to mechanical breakdowns, people started calling anything shoddy or trivial *Mickey Mouse*.

Using the following descriptions, identify the common words that have sprung from the sprightly pens of our cartoonists.

1. The name of H.T. Webster's wimpy comic-strip character, Casper _____, has become a synonym for a wimpy, unassertive man.

2. In a similar vein, some scholars assert that the term _____ _____ to designate a pathetically inept man, especially a soldier, owes its origin to the cartoon character created by George Baker.

3. In Elzie Segar's cartoon strip *Thimble Theatre*, which, when animated became *Popeye*, _____ was a mild-mannered, soft-spoken, lazy, parsimonious, and utterly gluttonous hamburger-wolfing straight man to Popeye.

4. The opposite of the mild-mannered creation in the preceding question is a _____, the comic book creation of writer Jerry Siegel and artist Joe Schuster. Faster than a speeding bullet! More powerful than a locomotive! Able to leap tall buildings in a single bound! _____ has become a person who exhibits extraordinary powers.

5. A common expression, "on the _____," meaning "not operating properly," may have started with one of our earliest comic strips, *The Katzenjammer Kids*. Two hyperactive German boys, Hans and

Fritz, caused all sorts of troubles for the Captain and other grown-ups in the story.

6. Two men of strikingly disparate height are dubbed _____ and _____. The original mustachioed twosome, one tall, one short, drawn by Bud Fisher, inhabited the first successful comic strip in America.

7. For more than nine decades, Blondie's husband has been creating culinary masterpieces in his kitchen, yet he doesn't appear to have gained an ounce (for which I envy him). This fellow carries a cornucopia of ingredients from the refrigerator to the kitchen table on his arms and head, and the massive repasts he concocts are now known as a _____ _____.

After centuries of telling and retelling, fairy tales have stepped out from pages in books and settled into the English language:

8. A golden-haired girl visits the home of three bears and chooses Baby Bear's chair, bed, and porridge because they are "just right." Today something in the _____ zone, such as our planet, is optimal, not at one extreme or the other.

9. A fairy-tale young woman is mistreated by her stepmother and stepsisters. With a little help from a fairy godmother, she attends a royal ball, marries a handsome prince, and lives happily ever after. Nowadays, a _____ ending is a happy ending, achieved after a long period of neglect and obscurity.

10. A fairy-tale princess pricks her finger on a spindle and sleeps for a hundred years until she is awakened by the kiss of a prince. Over time, these two characters have come to signify someone or something that lies dormant for years and an ideal male suitor: _____ and _____.

Answers

1. Milquetoast 2. Sad Sack 3. Wimpy 4. Superman 5. on the fritz
6. Mutt and Jeff 7. Dagwood sandwich 8. Goldilocks 9. Cinderella
10. Sleeping Beauty / Prince Charming

LITERARY MISCONCEPTIONS

"I hate soccer," wrote William F. Reed, "and I'm tired of being made to feel guilty about it. So there. I feel better now. Call me an ugly American, but please don't try to sell me on the World Cup."

In a *Newsday* piece published six months later, Timothy Phelps observed, "[Saddam Hussein's message] has been bolstered by his willingness to defy not only the ugly Americans, whose culture and political power threaten Arab moral values and independence as much as the Persians ever did ... "

What's wrong with the statements above? Look again at Reed's and Phelps's use of the epithets "ugly American" and "ugly Americans." Both writers employ the phrase to signify a citizen of the United States who has little appreciation for things foreign. Indeed, "ugly American" has become a catchphrase meaning "an American in a foreign country whose behavior is offensive to the people of that country."

Merriam-Webster traces "Ugly American" (capitalized in that dictionary) to *The Ugly American* (1958), a collection of stories written by William J. Lederer and Eugene Burdick.

Reed Phelps's and the dictionary's sense of the epithet constitutes one of the most universal of literary misconceptions in the English-speaking world—that an "ugly American" is one who exhibits uncomely behavior. In the title story of Lederer and Burdick's collection, the ugly American is a man named Homer Atkins, an engineer sent to Vietnam to work in heavy construction. The grease-spattered Atkins is indeed ugly in appearance (hence the

Ugly American), but he is also culturally sensitive, hardheaded, and honest about his task:

"Of course you've got good people out there in the boondocks, good hard-working people who are plenty savvy. But they don't want what you want yet. It takes time for that. That's why I recommend in my report that you start small, with little things. And then after you lick them, go on to bigger things. Hell, we could build dams and roads for you, but you don't have the skill or capacity or need for them now."

Ultimately, Atkins is assigned to the boondocks of Sarkhan, where, with the help of an "ugly Sarkhanese" named Jeepo, he invents and implements a man-powered water pump to lift the water from one terraced rice paddy to another in the Sarkhanese villages. So the original ugly American, with his integrity and pragmatic effectiveness, is anything but ugly in the sense of that term today.

Poor Homer Atkins, a literary allusion who has become an illusion. Of all the characters in *The Ugly American*, he is the most aware of the cultural context and needs of people in Southeast Asia. If he were real, he might sue for defamation of literary character.

Here are questions about other expressions, characters, and titles that were born from the tip of a pen and that are often misapplied in everyday parlance. Compare your answers with those that follow the questions.

1. What is "the lion's share"?
2. Who was Frankenstein?
3. Would you like to acquire "the Midas touch"?
4. What is the "immaculate conception," and where in the Bible do we find the phrase?

5. In a title such as *Apologia pro Vita Sua*, by Cardinal John Henry Newman, what does *Apologia* mean
6. In the expression "The hand that rocks the cradle rules the world," who is the cradle-rocker?

7. Does the saying "A rolling stone gathers no moss" support or criticize the wandering, knockabout life?

8. To what does the smithy refer in the famous opening lines of Henry Wadsworth Longfellow's "The Village Smithy"?:

> Under a spreading chestnut tree
> The village smithy stands.

Answers

1. In the original Aesop's fable, the Lion threatens the Fox, Jackal, and Wolf and ends up eating the entire stag. Literally, and literarily, "the lion's share" means the whole shebang, ball of wax, and shootin' match, not just a portion larger than anyone else's.

2. Frankenstein refers to the mad doctor (actually the young medical student) in Mary Wollstonecraft Shelley's classic horror novel. Old Zipperneck is properly alluded to as "Frankenstein's monster." Puristically, the cliché "creating a Frankenstein" makes no sense. In the novel, Dr. Frankenstein's creation is referred to as a "creature," "wretch," "fiend," "monster," "demon," and, in a single instance, "abortion."

3. Most people would because most people interpret the Midas touch to mean success in matters financial, the ability to make everything one touches turn to gold. In Greek mythology, King Midas was a monarch in Asia Minor who was granted the wish of the golden touch. The problem was that everything, including his food and drink, turned to gold. When even his beloved daughter became transmuted, he begged to have the gift withdrawn and had to bathe in the Pactolus River to remove what was a curse, not a blessing.

4. It is a misconception to believe that "the immaculate conception" refers to the birth of Jesus. Rather, it designates the doctrine that Mary was born without any taint of original sin. This doctrine was not declared by the Roman Catholic Church to be an article of faith until 1854, when Pope Pius IX issued the Bull *Ineffabilis Deus*.

Hence, the phrase "immaculate conception" does not appear in the Bible.

5. *Apologia* issues from a Late Latin word that means "a justification or defense," not "a statement of regret." *Apology* ultimately descends from the Greek *apologein*, "to tell fully," and in his *Apologia* Newman recounts his spiritual development.

6. In the old saw "the hand that rocks the cradle rules the world," just about everybody thinks that the hand is attached to mothers. But the cradle-rocker is God, as is evident from the original context of the line in "The Hand That Rules the World," by the nineteenth-century American poet Ross Wallace:

> They say that man is mighty,
> He governs land and sea.
> He wields a mighty sceptre
> O'er lesser powers that be;
> But a mightier power and stronger
> Man from his throne has hurled,
> For the hand that rocks the cradle
> Is the hand that rules the world.

7. Thomas Tusser's *A Hundred Points of Good Husbandrie* (1557) makes it clear that people who are always on the move and don't settle down will never become prosperous:

> The stone that is rolling can gather no moss,
> For master and servant oft changing is loss.

8. A smithy is a blacksmith's shop, not a blacksmith. The iron-worker is a smith, as the next two lines of Longfellow's poem indicate:

> The smith, a mighty man is he,
> With large and sinewy hands.

ALL'S WELL THAT ENDS WELL

"L—d, said my mother, what is all this story about?—A COCK and a BULL, said Yorick—And one of the best kind I ever heard" is the sprightly ending of Laurence Sterne's *Tristram Shandy*. Cock and bull stories are so called because ancient fables were filled with birds and animals walking and talking and acting like people.

The problem with stories, be they cock and bull or not, is that they require to be wound up. In that process, some stories go dead, while others conclude memorably. "Great is the art of the beginning, but greater the art is of ending," wrote Thomas Fuller.

Here are the closing sentences from famous works of literature.

Using the list that follows, select the title of each work and the name of each author.

1. But I reckon I got to light out for the Territory ahead of the rest because Aunt Sally she's going to adopt me and sivilize me and I can't stand it. I been there before.

2. After all, tomorrow is another day.

3. So we beat on, boats against the current, borne back ceaselessly into the past.

4. Villains! I shrieked, dissemble no more! I admit the deed!—tear up the planks! —here! here!—it is the beating of his hideous heart!

5. They endured.

6. They don't know we're not allowed to use magic at home. I'm going to have a lot of fun with Dudley this summer.

7. Don't ever tell anybody anything. If you do, you start missing everybody.

8. It is a far, far better thing that I do, than I have ever done; it is a far, far better rest that I go to, than I have ever known.

9. So I awoke, and behold, it was a dream.

10. I lingered round them, under that benign sky: watched the moths fluttering among the heath and harebells: listened to the soft wind breathing through the grass; and wondered how anyone could ever imagine unquiet slumbers for the sleepers in that quiet earth.

11. That might be the subject of a new story—but our present story is ended.

12. Vale.

13. There were three thousand six hundred and fifty-three days like this in his sentence, from reveille to lights out. The three extra ones were because of the leap years.

14. There is more day to dawn. The sun is but a morning star.

15. Nowadays the world is lit by lightning! Blow out your candles, Laura—and so goodbye ...

Authors	Titles
1. Emily Brontë	*The Adventures of Huckleberry Finn*
2. John Bunyan	*Catcher in the Rye*
3. Miguel de Cervantes	*Crime and Punishment*
4. Charles Dickens	*Don Quixote*
5. Fyodor Dostoevsky	*The Glass Menagerie*
6. William Faulkner	*Gone with the Wind*
7. F. Scott Fitzgerald	*The Great Gatsby*
8. Margaret Mitchell	*Harry Potter and the Sorcerer's Stone*
9. Edgar Allan Poe	*One Day in the Life Of Ivan Denisovich*
10. J.K. Rowling	*The Pilgrim's Progress*
11. J.D. Salinger	*The Sound and the Fury*

12. Alexandr Solzhenitsyn   *A Tale of Two Cities*
13. Henry David Thoreau   *The Tell-Tale Heart*
14. Mark Twain   *Walden*
15. Tennessee Williams   *Wuthering Heights*

Answers

1. Mark Twain, *The Adventures of Huckleberry Finn*, 2. Margaret Mitchell, *Gone with the Wind* 3. F. Scott Fitzgerald, *The Great Gatsby* 4. Edgar Allan Poe. "The Tell-Tale Heart" 5. William Faulkner, *The Sound and the Fury*

6. J.K. Rowling, *Harry Potter and the Sorcerer's Stone* 7. J.D. Salinger, *The Catcher in the Rye* 8. Charles Dickens, *A Tale of Two Cities* 9. John Bunyan, *The Pilgrim's Progress* 10. Emily Brontë, *Wuthering Heights*

11. Fyodor Dostoevsky, *Crime and Punishment* 12. Miguel de Cervantes, *Don Quixote* 13. Alexandr Solzhenitsyn, *One Day in the Life of Ivan Denisovich* 14. Henry David Thoreau, *Walden* 15. Tennessee Williams, *The Glass Menagerie*

STILL HOT OFF THE PRESS

Ezra Pound defined literature as "news that stays news." The plots spun out by many classic works of literature are as contemporary as today's headlines, especially as they are screamed in the tabloids. Just think what the *National Enquirer* and *Star* would do with the stories told in famous books if they had actually happened.

What literary plots are reflected in the following lurid headlines? Name the author who wrote each grisly tale.

1. VERONA TEENAGERS COMMIT DOUBLE SUICIDE; FAMILIES VOW TO END CLAN VENDETTA

2. CHICAGO CHAUFFEUR SMOTHERS BOSS'S DAUGHTER, THEN CUTS HER UP AND STUFFS HER IN FURNACE

3. GARAGE OWNER STALKS AFFLUENT BUSINESSMAN, THEN SHOTGUNS HIM IN HIS SWIMMING POOL

4. DOCTOR'S WIFE AND LOCAL MINISTER EXPOSED FOR CONCEIVING ILLEGITIMATE DAUGHTER

5. STUDENT CONFESSES TO AXE MURDER OF LOCAL PAWNBROKER AND ASSISTANT

6. MAD WOMAN LONG IMPRISONED IN ATTIC SETS HOUSE ON FIRE, THEN LEAPS TO DEATH

RICHARD LEDERER

7. FORMER SCHOOLTEACHER,
   FOUND TO HAVE BEEN PROSTITUTE,
   COMMITTED TO INSANE ASYLUM

8. GOVERNMENT OFFICIAL'S WIFE,
   BEARING COUNT'S CHILD,
   FLINGS SELF UNDER TRAIN

9. GHOSTS OF FORMER SERVANTS
   HAUNT GOVERNESS, CHILDREN

10. SKELETON OF WINE TASTER DISCOVERED
    BEHIND BRICK WALL IN MANSION CELLAR

11. ITINERANT FARMWORKER
    BREAKS WOMAN'S NECK
    THEN MERCY-KILLED BY BUDDY

12. MAYOR FOUND TO HAVE AUCTIONED
    OFF WIFE AND DAUGHTER TO SAILOR

13. STEPMOTHER STRANGLES HER BABY
    TO PROVE LOVE FOR HER STEPSON;
    BOTH GIVE THEMSELVES UP

14. SMITTEN BY MULTIPLE PERSONALITY DISORDER,
    PROMINENT LONDON DOCTOR KILLS SELVES

15. MAROONED ON CORAL ISLAND,
    BRITISH PREPPIES KILL EACH OTHER

16. WOMAN RAISED IN CONVENT,
    CAUGHT IN WEB OF SEX
    AND DEBT, TAKES ARSENIC

17. PRINCE ACQUITTED OF KILLING MOTHER
   IN REVENGE FOR MURDER OF HIS FATHER

18. WOMAN KNITS WARDROBES
   DURING PUBLIC EXECUTIONS

19. LORD OF MANOR FRIGHTENED TO DEATH
   BY GIANT PHOSPHORESCENT DOG

20. ADULTERERS SURVIVE DUAL SUICIDE PACT;
   ATTEMPTED TO RAM THEIR SLED INTO TREE

Answers

1. William Shakespeare, *Romeo and Juliet* 2. Richard Wright, *Native Son* 3. F. Scott Fitzgerald, *The Great Gatsby* 4. Nathaniel Hawthorne, *The Scarlet Letter* 5. Fyodor Dostoevsky, *Crime and Punishment*

6. Charlotte Brontë, *Jane Eyre* 7. Tennessee Williams, *A Streetcar Named Desire* 8. Leo Tolstoy, *Anna Karenina* 9. Henry James, *The Turn of the Screw* 10. Edgar Allan Poe, "The Cask of Amontillado"

11. John Steinbeck, *Of Mice and Men* 12. Thomas Hardy, *The Mayor of Casterbridge* 13. *Eugene O'Neill, Desire Under the Elms* 14. *Robert Louis Stevenson, The Strange Case of Dr. Jekyll and Mr. Hyde* 15. William Golding, *Lord of the Flies*

16. Gustave Flaubert, *Madame Bovary* 17. Aeschylus, *Eumenides* (in the *Oresteia*) 18. Charles Dickens, *A Tale of Two Cities* 19. Arthur Conan Doyle, "The Hound of the Baskervilles" 20. Edith Wharton, *Ethan Frome*

BOOKS IN THE NEWS

When the Boston Red Sox won the first two games of a World Series in alien Shea Stadium and then lost the next two games at Fenway Park, the Boston headline wept, THERE WAS NO JOY IN FENWAY.

That headline paraphrases the ballad "Casey at the Bat," composed by Ernest Lawrence Thayer:

> Oh! somewhere is this favored land
> The sun is shining bright,
> The band is playing somewhere,
> And somewhere hearts are light.
> And somewhere men are laughing,
> And somewhere children shout,
> But there is no joy in Mudville—
> Mighty Casey has struck out.

A rich vein of modern-day allusion is literature. Each quotation that follows appeared in a newspaper or magazine, and each alludes to a literary work.

Identify each source.

1. People like David Frum are deadweight, wannabe Cassandras who foretell disaster but who fail to urge us to "rage against the dying of the light" of American democracy.

2. For many Americans, April is indeed the cruelest month because it contains the deadline for filing tax returns to the Internal Revenue Service.

3. In this pandemic, nursing homes are the perfect storm for the spread of the coronavirus.

4. Happy newsrooms are all alike, but every unhappy newsroom is unhappy in its own way. And in this moment of cultural reckoning, most American newsrooms are unhappy places.

5. Gaslighting has been a major feature of American civic life since 2016, but in 2020 it reached new heights of outlandishness, making many of us feel as if we'd been pushed to the other side of the looking glass.

6. "CBS Sunday Morning" comes into our living rooms on little cat feet.

7. Is it the best of times and the worst of times for San Diego libraries?

8. We live in this world in which the current quarter never seems to pan out as well as people thought it would, and then they say the upturn will be in the next quarter. It's like waiting for Godot.

9. Life in Azerbaijan is nasty, brutish, and short.

10. He stoppeth one in three (from a story about a hapless hockey goalie).

Answers

1. Cassandra, daughter of Priam and Hecuba in the *Iliad*, possessed the gift of prophesy, but nobody believed what she predicted. In "Do Not Go Gentle Into That Good Night," poet Dylan Thomas urges his father, "Do not go gentle into that good night,/Old age should burn and rage at close of day;/Rage, rage against the dying of the light."

2. "April is the cruelest month" is the opening line of T.S. Eliot's bleak poem *The Wasteland*.

3. *The Perfect Storm* is the title of a sea novel by Sebastian Junger.

4. Leo Tolstoy's *Anna Karenina* opens with "Happy families are all alike; every unhappy family is unhappy in its own way."

5. *Through the Looking-Glass, and What Alice Found There* is Lewis Carroll's sequel to *Alice's Adventures in Wonderland.* Alice again enters an outlandish world, this time through a mirror.

6. Carl Sandberg's poem "Fog" opens with "The fog comes on little cat feet."

7. Charles Dickens's *A Tale of Two Cities* opens with "It was the best of times, it was the worst of times."

8. Samuel Beckett's tragi-comic play *Waiting for Godot* is about two tramps waiting on a country road by a leafless tree for somebody named Godot. And waiting. And waiting. And waiting.

9. In Thomas Hobbes's *Leviathan,* the author asserts that life is "solitary, poor, nasty, brutish, and short."

10. An ingenious reference to Samuel Taylor Coleridge's poem "The Rime of the Ancient Mariner," in which the Mariner "stoppeth one in three" listeners to spool out his tale of crime and punishment over and over and over again.

TITLES

HEAVYWEIGHT TITLES

When writers conjure up titles for their works, they draw their ideas from many sources, including the works of writers who have come before them. Take Ernest Hemingway as an example. He wrote a big novel about a man's personal commitment to a struggling people during the Spanish Civil War, and he sought a title that would express the interdependence of all human beings. Hemingway eventually found that title in a meditation composed by the early seventeenth-century writer John Donne: "Any man's death diminishes me because I am involved in mankind, and therefore never send to know for whom the bell tolls; it tolls for thee."

Hemingway named his novel *For Whom the Bell Tolls.*

Here are thirty literary passages, each of which inspired the title of another famous literary work that came after. Identify the title sparked by each passage and the author of each work.

1. Mine eyes have seen the glory
    Of the coming of the Lord;
    He is tramping out the vintage
    Where the grapes of wrath are stored.
-Julia Ward Howe, "Battle Hymn of the Republic"

2. What happens to a dream deferred?
    Does it dry up
    Like a raisin in the sun?
-Langston Hughes, "Harlem"

3. John Brown's body
   Lies a-moldering in the grave,
   His soul goes marching on.
-folk song, "John Brown's Body"

4. Humpty Dumpty sat on a wall:
   Humpty Dumpty had a great fall.
   All the King's horses
   And all the King's men
   Couldn't put Humpty together again.
-nursery rhyme, "Humpty Dumpty"

5. Look homeward, Angel, now, and melt with ruth:
   And o ye dolphins, waft the hapless youth.
-John Milton, "Lycidas"

6. Far from the madding crowd's ignoble strife,
   Their sober wishes never learned to stray;
   Along the cool sequestered vale of life
   They kept the noiseless tenor of their way.
-Thomas Gray,"Elegy Written in a Country Churchyard"

7. It Beareth the name of Vanity-Fair, because the town where
   'tis kept is lighter than Vanity.
-John Bunyan, *The Pilgrim's Progress*

8. Away! away! for I will fly to thee,
   Not charioted by Bacchus and his pards,
   But on the viewless wings of poesy,
   Though the dull brain perplexes and retards
   Already with thee! tender is the night.
-John Keats, "Ode to a Nightingale"

9. The best laid schemes o' mice an' men,

Gang aft a-gley,
An' lea'e us naught but grief an' pain
For promised joy!
-Robert Burns, "To a Mouse"

10. It is not a carol of joy or glee,
But a prayer that he sends from his heart's deep core,
But a plea, that upward to heaven he flings—
I know why the caged bird sings!
-Paul Laurence Dunbar, "Sympathy"

11. Go down Moses, way down to Egypt land.
Tell old Pharaoh: Let my people go.
-spiritual, "When Israel Was in Egypt's Land"

12. Of arms and the man I sing
-Virgil, *Aeneid*

13. One flew east, one flew west,
One flew over the cuckoo's nest.
-children's counting rhyme

14. "You and me, we've made a separate peace."
-Ernest Hemingway, "A Very Short Story"

15. I have forgot much, Cynara! gone with the wind,
Flung roses, roses riotously with the throng,
Dancing, to put thy pale, lost lilies out of mind.
-Ernest Dowson, "Cynara"

16. Turning and turning in the widening gyre
The falcon cannot hear the falconer;
Things fall apart; the centre cannot hold;
Mere anarchy is loosed upon the world.
-William Butler Yeats, "The Second Coming"

17. Gentlemen-rankers out on the spree,
    Damned from here to Eternity,
    God ha' mercy on such as we,
    Baa! Yah! Bah!
-Rudyard Kipling, "Gentlemen-Rankers"

18. Seize the day, put no trust in the morrow!
-Horace, *Odes,* Book I, Ode xi

19. And what rough beast, its hour come round at last,
    Slouches towards Bethlehem to be born?
-William Butler Yeats, "The Second Coming"

20. I will find out where she has gone
    And kiss her lips and take her hands;
    And walk among long dappled grass,
    And pluck till time and times are done
    The silver apples of the moon,
    The golden apples of the sun.
-William Butler Yeats, "The Song of Wandering Aengus"

21. Cast a cold eye
    On life, on death.
    Horseman, pass by!
-William Butler Yeats, "Under Ben Bulben"

22. Well this side of Paradise! ...
    There's little comfort in the wise.
-Rupert Brooke, "Tiare Tahiti"

23. Oh, beat the drum slowly and play the fife lowly,
    And play the dead march as you carry me along;
    Take me to the green valley, there lay the sod o'er me,
    For I'm a young cowboy, and I know I've done wrong.
-folksong, "The Cowboy's Lament"

24. Though nothing can bring back the hour
   Of splendor in the grass, of glory in the flower.
-William Wordsworth, "Intimations of Immortality"

25. Between the dark and the daylight,
   When the night is beginning to lower,
   Comes a pause in the day's occupations
   That is known as the Children's Hour.
-Henry Wadsworth Longfellow, "The Children's Hour"

26. I [Death] was astonished to see him in Baghdad, for I had an
   appointment with him tomorrow in Samarra.
-W. Somerset Maugham, *Sheppey*

27. When a true genius appears in the world, you may know him
   by this sign that the dunces are all in confederacy against
   him.
-Jonathan Swift, "Thoughts on Various Subjects"

28. A Book of Verses underneath the Bough,
   A Jug of Wine, a Loaf of Bread—and thou
   Beside me singing in the Wilderness—
   Oh, Wilderness were Paradise enou!
-Edward FitzGerald, *Rubaiyat of Omar Khayyam*

29. Go tell it on the mountain,
   Over the hills and everywhere,
   Go tell it on the mountain
   That Jesus Christ is born.
-African American spiritual

30. Two roads diverged in a wood, and I—
   I took the one less traveled by,
   And that has made all the difference.
-Robert Frost, "The Road Not Taken"

Answers

1. John Steinbeck, *The Grapes of Wrath* 2. Lorraine Hansberry, *A Raisin in the Sun* 3. Stephen Vincent Benét, *John Brown's Body* 4. Robert Penn Warren, *All the King's Men* 5. Thomas Wolfe, *Look Homeward, Angel*

6. Thomas Hardy, *Far from the Madding Crowd* 7. William Makepeace Thackeray, *Vanity Fair* 8. F. Scott Fitzgerald, *Tender Is the Night* 9. John Steinbeck, *Of Mice and Men* 10. Maya Angelou, *I Know Why the Caged Bird Sings*

11. William Faulkner, *Go Down, Moses* 12. George Bernard Shaw, *Arms and the Man* 13. Ken Kesey, *One Flew Over the Cuckoo's Nest* 14. John Knowles, *A Separate Peace* 15. Margaret Mitchell, *Gone With the Wind*

16. Chinua Achebe, *Things Fall Apart*, also Robert B. Parker, *The Widening Gyre* 17. James Jones, *From Here to Eternity* 18. Saul Bellow, *Seize the Day* 19. Joan Didion, *Slouching Towards Bethlehem* 20. Ray Bradbury, *The Golden Apples of the Sun*, also Eudora Welty, *The Golden Apples*, and Marjorie Kinnan Rawlings, *Golden Apples*

21. Larry McMurtry, *Horseman, Pass By!* and Mary McCarthy, *Cast a Cold Eye* 22. F. Scott Fitzgerald, *This Side of Paradise* 23. Mark Harris, *Bang the Drum Slowly* 24. William Inge, *Splendor in the Grass* 25. Lillian Hellman, *The Children's Hour*

26. John O'Hara, *An Appointment in Samarra* 27. John Kennedy Toole, *A Confederacy of Dunces* 28. Eugene O'Neill, *Ah, Wilderness!* 29. James Baldwin, *Go Tell It on the* Mountain 30. M. Scott Peck, *The Road Less Traveled*

TITLE SEARCH

Master storyteller W. Somerset Maugham once revealed how he constructed his many titles: "A good title is apt, specific, attractive, new, and short." In addition to these recommended qualities, some famous titles possess intrigue by inviting us into the books they name so that we can find out what the title actually means.

For many readers, the title *One Flew Over the Cuckoo's Nest* seems to be no more than a casual reference to a children's folk rhyme. Others are drawn by the contradiction embedded in Ken Kesey's title into the eccentric, polarized world of the novel. Cuckoos do not build nests; they lay their eggs in the nests of other birds. The contradiction mirrors the central irrationality of the novel itself, in which the bars separating the sane and insane, saints and sinners, and watchers and watched waver and blur.

Answer each of the following questions to show how the meanings of literary titles are often revealed in the works they announce.

1. What is the prize in Shirley Jackson's story "The Lottery"?

2. Who is Charley in John Steinbeck's *Travels With Charley*?

3. In J.D. Salinger's novel, who is the catcher in *The Catcher in the Rye*, and why is he a catcher?

4. Why did George Orwell choose *Nineteen Eighty-Four* as title and year of his novel?

5. Who is Algernon in Daniel Keyes's *Flowers for Algernon*?

6. In Joseph Heller's World War II novel *Catch-22* what is catch-22?

7. In T.S. Eliot's play *Murder in the Cathedral*, who was murdered?

8. What is the profession in George Bernard Shaw's play *Mrs. Warren's Profession?*

9. In what army is Shaw's *Major Barbara* a soldier?

10. What are the two cities in Charles Dickens's *A Tale of Two Cities?*

11. Why did Samuel Butler name his utopia *Erewhon?*

12. In Gerard Manley Hopkins' poem "The Windhover" what is a windhover?

13. In Nathaniel Hawthorne's *The Scarlet Letter,* what is the letter and what does it stand for?

14. In the title of Karel Capek's play *R. U.R.* what do the letters signify

15. What does *wuthering* mean in Emily Brontë's title *Wuthering Heights?*

16. In Alexandr Solzhenitsyn's *The Gulag Archipelago,* what do *gulag* and *archipelago* mean?

17. In the title of H.G. Wells's social novel *Tono-Bungay* to what does Tono-Bungay refer?

18. What is the speaker's modest proposal in "A Modest Proposal," by Jonathan Swift?

19. In Robert Browning's "The Pied Piper of Hamelin" and Gerard Manley Hopkins' "Pied Beauty," what does *pied* mean?

20. In William Golding's novel, who or what is the *Lord of the Flies?*

21. What is the jungle in Upton Sinclair's *The Jungle?*

22. In Stendhal's *The Charterhouse of Parma,* what is a charterhouse?

23. In Arthur Conan Doyle's "The Five Orange Pips," what are pips?

24. In *Out of the Silent Planet* and *Perelandra,* what two planets is C.S. Lewis referring to in his titles?

25. What is the talisman in Walter Scott's *The Talisman?*

26. What is the lock in Alexander Pope's "The Rape of the Lock" and how was it "raped"?

27. What is the folly in Joseph Conrad's *Almayer's Folly?*

28. What is the name of the town in Thornton Wilder's play *Our Town?*

29. What is a scrivener in Herman Melville's story "Bartleby the Scrivener"?

30. What is the octopus in Frank Norris's *The Octopus?*

Answers

1. death by stoning 2. Steinbeck's pet poodle 3. Holden Caulfield, who hears the line in the Robert Burns song "If a body meet a body coming through the rye" as "If a body catch a body coming through the rye" 4. Orwell reversed the last two digits of 1948, the year in which he wrote much of the book, in order to show that within a single generation, democracy and freedom could be obliterated. 5. a laboratory rat

6. a military regulation that keeps the pilots in the story flying one suicidal mission after another 7. Thomas Becket, Archbishop of Canterbury 8. prostitution 9. the Salvation Army 10. London and Paris

11. It's *Nowhere* spelled backward—almost. 12. a kestrel hawk, which hovers so gracefully above the wind 13. *A*, adultery 14. "Rossum's Universal Robots." In 1921 Capek invented the word *robot*, from a Czech root meaning "to work," for his play. 15. the sound that wind makes blowing through trees

16. *Gulag* is an acronym for the Russian words "Chief Administration of Collective Labor Camps." An archipelago is a cluster of islands, in this case an analogy to the network of prison sites spread throughout Russia. 17. a drug, a phony cure-all 18. that the children of poor people be sold as food for the tables of the rich 19. multicolored, blotched 20. a pig's head on a stick, the devil, or perhaps the darkness of the human heart

21. Chicago's meat-packing district 22. a monastery 23. seeds 24. Earth and Venus 25. an amulet with curative powers

26. a lock of hair of a real-life Miss Arabella Fermor, snipped off by one Robert Lord Petre 27. a house 28. Grover's Corner, New Hampshire 29. a professional copyist or scribe 30. the railroad

Mary Ellen Chase gave her tall tale a very short title, *Harvey*. Harvey isn't a person; he's a six-foot-one-inch rabbit seen only by his companion, the eccentric Elwood P. Dowd. The play was almost called *Daisy*, as Chase's original conception was of a four-foot-tall canary with that name.

Other titles do not reveal characters by name. Provide the name of each character referred to in each title:

1. Victor Hugo's *The Hunchback of Notre Dame*
2. James Fenimore Cooper's *The Last of the Mohicans*
3. Robert Bolt's *A Man For All Seasons*
4. Oliver Goldsmith's *The Vicar of Wakefield*
5. D.H. Lawrence's *Lady Chatterley's Lover*

6. Edward Everett Hale's *The Man Without a Country*
7. Alexandre Dumas' *The Three Musketeers*
8. Fyodor Dostoevsky's *The Brothers Karamazov*
9. Louisa May Alcott's *Little Women*
10. Richard Wright's *Native Son*

11. H.G. Wells's *The Invisible Man*
12. Ralph Ellison's *Invisible Man*
13. Oliver Wendell Holmes's *The Autocrat of the Breakfast-Table*
14. John Webster's *The White Devil*
15. Rudyard Kipling's *Stalky and Co.*

16. Henry James's *The Portrait of a Lady*
17. Moliere's *The Miser*
18. James Fenimore Cooper's *The Pathfinder*

19. George S. Kaufman and Moss Hart's *The Man Who Came to Dinner*

20. James Joyce's *A Portrait of the Artist as a Young Man*

Answers

1. Quasimodo 2. Chingachgook and his son, Uncas 3. Thomas More 4. Dr. Charles Primrose 5. Oliver Mellors

6. Philip Nolan 7. Athos, Porthos, and Aramis 8. Dimitri, Ivan, Alyosha, and Smerdyakov 9. Meg, Jo, Beth, and Amy March 10. Bigger Thomas

11. Griffin 12. He is never named. 13. Oliver Wendell Holmes 14. Vittoria Corombona 15. Arthur Lionel Corkran

16. Isabel Archer 17. Harpagon 18. Natty Bumppo 19. Sheridan Whiteside 20. Stephen Dedalus

PLAYING THE NUMBERS GAME

When a number of books he had lent were not returned, Walter Scott quipped, "My friends may not be good in mathematics, but they are excellent book-keepers." Authors are sometimes unmathematical, but the numbers they place in some of their titles are often significant to the stories themselves.

In Ray Bradbury's *Fahrenheit 451*, for example, the title turns out to be the temperature at which book paper ignites, an important figure in a society that employs firemen not to save houses but to burn down houses—houses suspected of containing books.

The working title for Joseph Heller's modern classic novel about the mindlessness of war was *Catch-18*, a reference to a military regulation that keeps the pilots in the story flying one suicidal mission after another. The only way to be excused from flying such missions is to be declared insane, but asking to be excused is proof of a rational mind and bars excuse.

Shortly before the appearance of Heller's book in 1961, Leon Uris's *Mila 18* was published. To avoid confusion with the title of Uris's war novel, Heller and his editor decided to change *Catch-18* to *Catch-22*. The choice turned out to be both fortunate and fortuitous as the *22* more rhythmically and symbolically captures the double duplicity of both the military regulation itself and the bizarre world that Heller shapes in his novel.

During the more than sixty years since its literary birth, *catch-22* has come to mean any predicament in which we are caught coming and going and in which the very nature of the problem denies and defies its solution. So succinctly does *catch-22* embody the push-me-pull-you absurdity of modern life that the word has become the most frequently employed and deeply embedded allusion from all of twentieth-century American literature.

Using the name of each author and each embedded number, provide the title of each work. Let's start with the numbers one to ten.

1. Alexandr Solzhenitsyn (1)	19. Luigi Pirandello (6)
2. Ken Kesey (1)	20. A.A. Milne (6)
3. Judy Blume (1)	21. W. Somerset Maugham (6)
4. T.H. White (1)	22. Nadine Gordimer (6)
5. William Shakespeare (2)	23. Nathaniel Hawthorne (7)
6. Charles Dickens (2)	24. Nicholas Meyer (7)
7. Doris Lessing (2)	25. T.E. Lawrence (7)
8. Richard Henry Dana (2)	26. Aeschylus (7)
9. Alexandre Dumas (3)	27. Fletcher Knebel (7)
10. Anton Chekhov (3)	28. Louisa May Alcott (8)
11. Audrey Niffenegger (3)	29. John O'Hara (8)
12. Yann Martel (3.1519 . .	30. Richard Wright (8)
13. T.S. Eliot (4)	31. Dorothy L. Sayers (9)
14. Maeve Binchy (4)	32. J.D. Salinger (9)
15. Arthur Conan Doyle (4)	33. Margaret Atwood (9)
16. Kurt Vonnegut (5)	34. Agatha Christie (10)
17. Ernest Hemingway (5)	35. Gretchen McNeil (10)
18. Arthur Conan Doyle (5)	36. John Reed (10)

Answers

1. *One Day in the Life of Ivan Denisovich* 2. *One Flew Over the Cuckoo's Nest* 3. *The One in the Middle Is the Green Kangaroo* 4. *The Once and Future King*

5. *Two Gentleman of Verona, The Two Noble Kinsmen* (co-written with John Fletcher) 6. *A Tale of Two Cities* 7. *A Man with Two Women* 8. *Two Years Before the Mast*

9. *The Three Musketeers* 10. *The Three Sisters* 11. *The Three Incestuous Sisters* 12. *Three Soldiers*

13. *The Story of Pi* 14. *Four Quartets* 15. "The Sign of Four" 16. *Slaughterhouse-Five*

17. *The Fifth Column* 18. "The Five Orange Pips" 19. *Six Characters in Search of an Author* 20. *Now We Are Six*

21. *The Moon and Sixpence* 22. *The House of the Seven Gables* 23. *The Seven-Per-Cent Solution* 24. *Seven Against Thebes*

25. *Seven Pillars of Wisdom* 26. *Seven Against Thebes* 27. *Seven Days in May* 28. *Eight Cousins*

29. *Butterfield 8* 30. *Eight Men* 31. *The Nine Tailors* 32. *Nine Stories*

33. *Nine Tales* 34. *Ten Little Indians* 35. *Ten* 36. *Ten Days That Shook the World*

Using the name of each author and each embedded number from twelve to a million, provide the title of each work.

1. Ursula K. Le Guin (12)
2. Solomon Northrup (12)
3. Reginald Rose (12)
4. Ruth Rendell (13)
5. Leon Uris (18)
6. Jodi Picoult (19)
7. A.E. Housman (21)
8. John Buchan (39)
9. John Dos Passos (42)
10. Thomas Pynchon (49)
11. Harold Robbins (79)
12. Jules Verne (80)
13. Helene Hanff (84)
14. Victor Hugo (93)
15. Gabriel Garcia Marquez (100)
16. Amy Tan (100)
17. Dodie Smith (101)
18. Marquis de Sade (120)
19. Jane Smiley (1,000)
20. Arabian folk tales (1,001)
21. Arthur C. Clarke (2,001)
22. Jules Verne (20,000)
23. Ernest Hemingway (50,000)
24. Mark Twain (1,000,000)
25. James Frey (1,000,000)

Answers

1. *The Wind's Twelve Quarters* 2. *Twelve Years a Slave* 3. *Twelve Angry Men* 4. *Thirteen Steps Down* 5. *Mila 18*

6. *Nineteen Minutes* 7. "When I was One-and-Twenty" 8. *The Thirty-Nine Steps* 9. *The 42nd Parallel* 10. *The Crying of Lot 49*

11. *79 Park Avenue* 12. *Around the World in Eighty Days* 13. *84, Charing Cross Road* 14. *Ninety-Three* 15. *One Hundred Years of Solitude*

16. *The Hundred Secret Senses* 17. *101 Dalmatians* 18. *One Hundred Twenty Days of Sodom* 19. *A Thousand Acres* 20. *The Thousand and One Nights*

21. *2001: A Space Odyssey* 22. *Twenty Thousand Leagues Under the Sea* 23. "Fifty Grand" 24. "The £1,000,000 Bank-Note" 25. *A Million Little Pieces*

One of the most enigmatic of number mysteries occurs in a text, not a title. What may well be the most famous of O. Henry's short stories, "The Gift of the Magi" (1906), begins with this sentence: "One dollar and eighty-seven cents. That was all. And sixty cents of it was in pennies."

Do we have here yet another creative but impractical author who has trouble with his math? It is, of course, impossible to make up $1.87 if sixty (rather than sixty-two) cents of it is in pennies.

But not so fast. Turns out that, in the United States, two – and three-cent pieces were struck during the late nineteenth century and remained in circulation for decades after. Thus, it would have been quite possible in O. Henry's America to have a dollar and eighty-seven cents that did not include any pennies at all.

ALLITERATURE

Alliteration is the occurrence, within a line or phrase, of words having the same initial sound. It's a device that many writers employ to create a treasure trove of tried-and-true, bread-and-butter, bigger-and-better, bright-eyed and bushy-tailed, do-or-die, footloose-and-fancy-free, larger-than-life, cream-of-the-crop titles.

Best-selling American novelist Janet Evanovich is the queen of alliterative titles, including *Back to the Bedroom*, *Naughty Neighbors*, and *The Rocky Road to Romance*. Add to those her numerical titles, such as *Sizzling Sixteen*, *Smokin' Seventeen*, *Explosive Eighteen*, *Notorious Nineteen*, and *Takedown Twenty*.

Using the clues of author and alliterated letter, identify the following alliterary works whose titles employ "apt alliteration's artful aid":

1. Frank McCourt (A)
2. John Dryden (A)
3. Herman Melville (B)
4. Richard Wright (B)
5. Anna Sewell (B)
6. Mary Norton (B)
7. Charles Dickens (C)
8. Dodie Smith (C)
9. Rudyard Kipling (C)
10. Kurt Vonnegut (C)
11. Mary Stewart (C)
12. Stephen Vincent Benét (D)
13. George Eliot (D)
14. P.D. James (D)
15. Ambrose Bierce (D)
16. Kathy Reichs (D)
17. John Steinbeck (E)
18. Erica Jong (F)
19. Mary O'Hara (F)
20. F. Scott Fitzgerald (G)
21. Gillian Flynn (G)
22. George Bernard Shaw (H)
23. John Patrick (H)
24. Shirley Jackson (H)
25. Dorothy L. Sayers (H)
26. William Wordsworth (I)

27. Samuel Taylor
Coleridge (K)
28. William Shakespeare (L)
29. Irving Stone (L)
30. Walter Scott (L)
31. Eugene O'Neill (L)
32. Frank Harris (L)
33. A.R. Gurney (L)
34. John Steinbeck (M)
35. Thomas Mann (M)
36. Herman Wouk (M)
37. Eugene O'Neill (M)
38. Victoria Holt (M)
39. Mikhail Bulgakov (M)
40. Muriel Spark (M)
41. Charles Dickens (N)
42. Jane Austen (P)
43. Charles Dickens (P)
44. Grace Metalious (P)
45. James Barrie (P)
46. Mark Twain (P)

47. John Bunyan (P)
48. Edgar Allan Poe (P)
49. Kurt Vonnegut (P)
50. Jean Auel (P)
51. John Updike (R)
52. Arthur Conan Doyle (S)
53. Richard Brinsley
Sheridan (S)
54. Joseph Conrad (S)
55. Jane Austen (S)
56. Rachel Carson (S)
57. Simone de Beauvoir (S)
58. Toni Morrison (S)
59. T.H. White (S)
60. J.R.R. Tolkien (T)
61. Nathaniel Hawthorne (T)
62. Kenneth Grahame (W)
63. H.G. Wells (W)
64. Maxine Hong
Kingston (W)
65. Herman Wouk (W)

Answers

1. *Angela's Ashes* 2. *Absalom and Achitophel* 3. *Billy Budd* 4. *Black Boy* 5. *Black Beauty*

6. *Bedknobs and Broomsticks* 7. *A Christmas Carol* 8. *I Capture the Castle* 9. *Captains Courageous* 10. *Cat's Cradle*

11. *The Crystal Cave* 12. *"The Devil and Daniel Webster"* 13. *Daniel Deronda* 14. *Devices and Desires* 15. *The Devil's Dictionary*

16. *Déjà Dead* 17. *East of Eden* 18. *Fear of Flying* 19. *My Friend Flicka* 20. *The Great Gatsby*

21. *Gone Girl* 22. *Heartbreak House* 23. *The Hasty Heart* 24. *The Haunting of Hill House* 25. *Hangman's Holiday*

26. "Intimations of Immortality" 27. "Kubla Khan" 28. *Love's Labour's Lost* 29. *Lust for Life* 30. *The Lady of the Lake*

31. *Lazarus Laughed* 32. *My Life and Loves* 33. *Love Letters* 34. *Of Mice and Men* 35. *The Magic Mountain*

36. *Marjorie Morningstar* 37. *A Moon for the Misbegotten* 38. *Momento Mori* 39. *The Master and Margarita* 40. *Mistress of Mellyn*

41. *Nicholas Nickleby* 42. *Pride and Prejudice* 43. *The Pickwick Papers* 44. *Peyton Place* 45. *Peter Pan*

46. *The Prince and the Pauper* 47. *The Pilgrim's Progress* 48. "The Pit and the Pendulum" 49. *Player Piano* 50. *The Plains of Passage*

51. *Rabbit, Run, Rabbit Is Rich, Rabbit Redux* 52. *A Study in Scarlet* 53. *The School for Scandal* 54. "The Secret Sharer" 55. *Sense and Sensibility*

56. *The Silent Spring* 57. *The Second Sex* 58. *Song of Solomon* 59. *The Sword in the Stone* 60. *The Two Towers*

61. *Twice-Told Tales* 62. *The Wind in the Willows* 63. *War of the Worlds* 64. *The Warrior Woman* 65. *The Winds of War*

As long as you're being so alliterate, identify the alliteratively named authors who wrote the following works:

1. *A Walk in the Woods* (B)
2. *The Lace Reader* (B)
3. *The Dwelling Place* (C)
4. *Robinson Crusoe* (D)
5. *Rebecca* (D)

6. *Fried Green Tomatoes at the Whistle Stop Cafe* (F)
7. *The Power and the Glory* (G)
8. *The Tin Drum* (G)
9. *Siddhartha* (H)
10. *Ulysses* (J)

11. *From Here to Eternity* (J)
12. *The Autobiography of an Ex-Colored Man* (J)
13. *Gods in Alabama* (J)
14. *The Heretic's Daughter* (K)
15. *One Flew Over the Cuckoo's Nest* (K)

16. *How the West Was Won* (L)

17. *The Girls* (L) 18. *The Giver* (L)

19. *Gone With the Wind* (M)

20. *The Group* (M)

21. *Growing Up in New Guinea* (M)

22. *Pomegranate Soup* (M)

23. *Uprooted* (N)

24. *Portobello* (R)

25. *Cost* (R)

26. *Master of the Game* (S)

27. *The Giving Tree* (S)

28. *The Lovers* (V)

29. *Leaves of Grass* (W)

30. *Lyrical Ballads* (W)

Answers

1. Bill Bryson 2. Brunonia Barry 3. Catherine Cookson 4. Daniel Defoe 5. Daphne Du Maurier

6. Fanny Flagg 7. Graham Greene 8. Gunter Grass 9. Hermann Hesse 10. James Joyce

11. James Jones 12. James Weldon Johnson 13. Joshilyn Jackson 14. Kathleen Kent 15. Ken Kesey

16. Louis L'Amour 17. Lori Lansens 18. Lois Lowry 19. Margaret Mitchell 20. Mary McCarthy

21. Margaret Mead 22. Marsha Mehran 23. Naomi Novik 24. Ruth Rendell 25. Roxana Robinson

26. Sidney Sheldon 27. Shel Silverstein 28. Vendela Vida 29. Walt Whitman 30. William Wordsworth

THE SPECTRUM

British poet and satirist Hilaire Belloc wrote as his epitaph:

> When I am dead, I hope it may be said,
> "His sins were scarlet, but his books were read."

Belloc is little-read today, alas; but, picking up on his waggish pun, a number of books are black and white and read all over—and, like Joseph's coat of many colors, yellow and gold and silver and blue and purple and scarlet and green and orange and gray.

In the spectrum of literature, colors play an important role in the names of books. In Bruce Catton's classic study of the Civil War, *The Blue and the Gray*, the colors, of course, signify the two sides in the conflict. In *The Red and the Black,* Stendahl creates a psychological study of the self-absorbed Julien Sorel. The two colors in the novel's title represent the military and the clergy, the two paths open to a young man of the upper class.

I'll roll out the red carpet and award you a blue ribbon and gold star if you can get your gray matter to identify the colorful titles created by the following authors. Let's start with the colors of the rainbow in the order they appear in nature.

Red
1. Sandra Brown
2. Stephen Crane
3. Tom Clancy
4. Arthur Conan Doyle
5. James Jones

6. Herman Melville
7. Edgar Allan Poe
8. John Steinbeck

Orange
9. Anthony Burgess

10. Arthur Conan Doyle
11. Claire Fuller
12. Piper Kerman

Yellow
13. Charlotte P. Gilman
14. Fred Gipson
15. Aldous Huxley

Green
16. Marc Connelly
17. Fannie Flagg
18. Elizabeth Goudge
19. W.H. Hudson
20. Stephen King
21. Richard Llewellyn
22. Robin Moore
23. L.M. Montgomery

24. Dr. Seuss

Indigo
25. Alice Hoffman
26. Ntozake Shange

Blue
27. Mary Higgins Clark
28. Stephen Crane
29. Arthur Conan Doyle
30. William Least-Heat Moon
31. Toni Morrison
32. Nora Roberts
33. Danielle Steel

Violet
34. SJI Holliday
35. James Patterson

1. *Seeing Red* 2. *The Red Badge of Courage* 3. *The Hunt for Red October, Red Storm Rising, Red Rabbit* 4. "The Red-Headed League" 5. *The Thin Red Line*

6. *Redburn* 7. "Masque of the Red Death" 8. *The Red Pony* 9. *A Clockwork Orange* 10. "The Five Orange Pips"

11. *Bitter Orange* 12. *Orange Is the New Black* 13. "The Yellow Wallpaper" 14. *Old Yeller* 15. *Chrome Yellow*

16. *The Green Pastures* 17. *Fried Green Tomatoes at the Whistle Stop Cafe*

18. *Green Dolphin Street* 19. *Green Mansions* 20. *The Green Mile*

21. *How Green Was My Valley* 22. *The Green Berets* 23. *Anne of Green Gables* 24. *Green Eggs and Ham* 25. *Indigo* 26. *Sassafras* 27. *Two Little Girls in Blue*

28. "The Blue Hotel" 29. "The Blue Carbuncle" 30. *Blue Highways* 31. *The Bluest Eye* 32. *Chesapeake Blue*

33. *Cypress & Indigo* 34. *Violet* 35. *Violets Are Blue*

Now identify the books with colorful titles that are not in the rainbow spectrum:

Black
1. Lorene Cary
2. Ann Cleeves
3. Patricia Cornwell
4. Alexandre Dumas
5. John Howard Griffin
6. Edgar Allan Poe
7. Anna Sewell
8. Richard Wright

White
9. Don DeLillo
10. Joan Didion
11. Janet Fitch
12. Ernest Hemingway
13. Sarah Orne Jewett
14. D.H. Lawrence
15. Jack London
16. Herman Melville
17. Zadie Smith

Gray
18. E.L. James
19. Dorothy Rice
20. Ruta Sepetys
21. Oscar Wilde
22. Sloane Wilson

Silver
23. Patricia Briggs
24. Mary Mapes Dodge
25. Tayari Jones
26. C.S. Lewis

Purple
27. Zane Grey
28. Alice Walker

Scarlet
29. Arthur Conan Doyle
30. Nathaniel Hawthorne
31. Baroness Emmuska Orczy
32. Julia Peterkin
33. Alexandra Ripley

Gold
34. Ray Bradbury
35. Ian Fleming
36. Joseph Heller
37. Henry James
38. Carson McCullers
39. Edgar Allan Poe
40. Donna Tartt

Answers

1. *Black Ice* 2. *Raven Black* 3. *Black Notice* 4. *The Black Tulip* 5. *Black Like Me* 6. "The Black Cat" 7. *Black Beauty* 8. *Black Boy* 9. *White Noise* 10. *The White Album*

11. *White Oleander* 12. "Hills Like White Elephants" 13. "A White Heron" 14. *The White Peacock* 15. *White Fang* 16. *White Jacket* 17. *White Teeth* 18. *Fifty Shades of Grey* 19. *Gray is the New Black* 20. *Between Shades of Gray*

21. *The Picture of Dorian Gray* 22. *The Man in the Gray Flannel Suit* 23. *Silver Borne* 24. *Hans Brinker, or The Silver Skates* 25. *Silver Sparrow*

26. *The Silver Chair* 27. *Riders of the Purple Sage* 28. *The Color Purple* 29. *A Study in Scarlet* 30. *The Scarlet Letter*

31. *The Scarlet Pimpernel* 32. *Scarlet Sister Mary* 33. *Scarlett* 34. *The Golden Apples of the Sun* 35. *Goldfinger*

36. *Good as Gold* 37. *The Golden Bowl* 38. *Reflections in a Golden Eye* 39. "The Gold Bug" 40. *The Goldfinch*

THE BESTIARY

Animals are the main characters in much of world literature, and collections of these tales were often called bestiaries. This animated tradition stretches from Aesop's fables and the mock epic *Batrachomyomachia (Battle of the Frogs and Mice)*, attributed to Homer, to modern works, such as George Orwell's *Animal Farm*, satirizing Russia under Stalin. Even when animals are not central characters, they roam the titles of books such as Tennessee Williams's *The Glass Menagerie*, Edward Albee's *Zoo Story*, Stephen King's *Pet Sematary*, and Barbara Kingsolver's *Animal Dreams*.

As Walt Whitman reminds us in "Song of Myself," we have much to learn from animals:

> I think I could turn and live with animals,
> They are so placid and self contain'd,
> I stand and look at them long and long.

The authors listed below have composed titles in which mammals prowl. Identify each title.

1. Margaret Atwood
2. Jean Auel
3. John Barth
4. Margery Williams Bianco
5. Michael Blake
6. William Blake
7. Pierre Boulle
8. Lilian Jackson Braun
9. Robert Burns
10. Edgar Rice Burroughs
11. Agatha Christie
12. James Fenimore Cooper
13. Patricia Cornwell
14. Arthur Conan Doyle

15. T.S. Eliot
16. Louise Erdrich
17. William Faulkner
18. Alexandra Fuller
19. Sara Gruen
20. Thomas Harris
21. Robert Heinlein
22. Lillian Hellman
23. Hermann Hesse
24. Eugene Ionesco
25. Rudyard Kipling
26. Sofie Laguna
27. C.S. Lewis
28. Jack London
29. Alistair MacLean
30. Norman Mailer
31. David Mamet
32. Caroline McCullagh

33. Larry McMurtry
34. Eugene O'Neill
35. Jodi Picoult
36. Edgar Allan Poe
37. Bernard Pomerance
38. Katherine Anne Porter
39. Dr. Seuss
40. George Bernard Shaw
41. Irwin Shaw
42. Dodie Smith
43. John Steinbeck
44. Mary Stewart
45. Frank Stockton
46. John Updike
47. Kurt Vonnegut
48. Jeanette Walls
49. Tennessee Williams
50. Sarah Winman

Answers

1. *Cat's Eye* 2. *The Clan of the Cave Bear, Valley of Horses, The Mammoth Hunters* 3. *Giles Goat-Boy* 4. *The Velveteen Rabbit* 5. *Dances With Wolves*

6. "The Tiger," "The Lamb" 7. *Planet of the Apes* 8. *The Cat Who Could Read Backwards* 9. "To a Mouse" 10. *Tarzan of the Apes*

11. *The Mouse Trap* 12. *The Deerslayer* 13. *Isle of Dogs* 14. "The Hound of the Baskervilles" 15. *Old Possum's Book of Practical Cats*

16. *The Antelope's Bride* 17. "The Bear" 18. *Don't Let's Go to the Dogs Tonight* 19. *Water for Elephants* 20. *The Silence of the Lambs*

21. *The Cat Who Walks Through Walls* 22. *The Little Foxes* 23. *Steppenwolf* 24. *The Rhinoceros* 25. "The Elephant's Child"; "How the Camel Got Its Hump"; "How the Leopard Got Its Spots"; "How the Rhino Got Its Skin"

26. *The Eye of the Sheep* 27. *The Lion, the Witch, and the Wardrobe, The Horse and His Boy* 28. *The Sea Wolf* 29. *Ice Station Zebra* 30. *The Deer Park*

31. *American Buffalo* 32. *Quest for the Ivory Caribou* 33. *Horseman, Pass By* 34. *The Hairy Ape* 35. *Lone Wolf*

36. "The Black Cat" 37. *The Elephant Man* 38. *Pale Horse, Pale Rider* 39. *The Cat in the Hat* 40. *Androcles and the Lion*

41. *The Young Lions* 42. *101 Dalmatians* 43. *Of Mice and Men, The Red Pony* 44. *The Gabriel Hounds* 45. "The Lady or the Tiger" 46. *Rabbit, Run, Rabbit Redux, Rabbit is Rich* 47. *Welcome to the Monkey House, Cat's Cradle* 48. *Half-Broke Horses* 49. *Cat on a Hot Tin Roof* 50. *When God Was a Rabbit*

VEGGING OUT

Cavalier poet Andrew Marvell wooed his "Coy Mistress" by promising that

> my vegetable love should grow
> Vaster than empires and more slow.

Writers often pluck their titles from the plant kingdom, from Baroness Emmuska Orcz's *The Scarlet Pimpernel*, in which the pimpernel is actually an herb in the primrose family, to George Orwell's *Keep the Aspidistra Flying*, in which an aspidistra is an Asian plant of the lily family. Identify the herbs, flowers, fruits, vegetables, and plants growing in the titles of the fertile, cultivated books written by the following down-to-earth authors:

1. V.C. Andrews	14. Fannie Flagg
2. John Barth	15. Kenneth Grahame
3. Ray Bradbury	16. Joanne Greenburg
4. Richard Brautigan	17. Lorraine Hansberry
5. Erskine Caldwell	18. Nathaniel Hawthorne
6. Anton Chekhov	19. Ernest Hemingway
7. Roald Dahl	20. O. Henry
8. Arthur Conan Doyle	21. Henry James
9. Umberto Eco	22. Jean Kerr
10. James Ellroy	23. Daniel Keyes
11. Louise Erdrich	24. Joyce Kilmer
12. William Faulkner	25. Stephen King
13. Jane Fitch	26. Barbara Kingsolver

27. W. Somerset Maugham
28. Margaret Mead
29. Eugene O'Neill
30. J.D. Salinger
31. George Bernard Shaw
32. Betty Smith
33. John Steinbeck

34. Jean Toomer
35. Mark Twain
36. Joseph Wambaugh
37. Walt Whitman
38. Laura Ingalls Wilder
39. Tennessee Williams
40. Paul Zindel

Answers

1. *Flowers in the Attic* 2. *The Sot-Weed Factor* 3. *Dandelion Wine, The Golden Apples of the Sun* 4. *In Watermelon Sugar* 5. *Tobacco Road*

6. *The Cherry Orchard,* "Gooseberries" 7. *James and the Giant Peach* 8. "The Five Orange Pips" 9. *The Name of the Rose* 10. *The Black Dahlia*

11. *The Beet Queen* 12. "A Rose for Emily," *A Green Bough* 13. *White Oleander* 14. *Fried Green Tomatoes at the Whistle Stop Cafe* 15. *The Wind in the Willows*

16. *I Never Promised You a Rose Garden* 17. *A Raisin in the Sun* 18. *Mosses from an Old Manse* 19. *Across the River and Into the Trees* 20. *Cabbages and Kings*

21. *On the Banks of Plum Creek* 22. *Please Don't Eat the Daisies* 23. *Daisy Miller* 24. *Flowers for Algernon* 25. "Trees"

26. *Children of the Corn* 27. "The Lotus Eater" 28. *Blackberry Winter* 29. 30. *Desire Under the Elms*

31. *The Catcher in the Rye* 32. *The Apple Cart* 33. *A Tree Grows in Brooklyn* 34. *The Grapes of Wrath* 34. *Cane* 35. *The Adventures of Huckleberry Finn*

36. *The Onion Field* 37. *Leaves of Grass* 38. *On the Banks of Plum Creek* 39. *The Rose Tattoo, Twenty-Seven Wagons Full of Cotton* 40. *The Effect of Gamma Rays on Man-in-the-Moon Marigolds*

The Game is the Name

One of the first things that each of us acquires when we enter this world is a name, and this name becomes the badge of our individuality. As poet James Russell Lowell wrote, "There is more force in names than most men dream of." Lewis Carroll recognized that force when he had Humpty Dumpty say to Alice, "My name means the shape I am—and a good handsome shape it is, too."

In their best-known form, the titles of many works of literature consist entirely of a character's first and last name. Charles Dickens used this formula to title five of his novels *Barnaby Rudge, David Copperfield, Martin Chuzzlewit, Nicholas Nickleby,* and *Oliver Twist.*

Embedded in the two columns below are thirty titles, each fabricated from a first and last name. Match each first name with each surname and identify the author of each work.

1. Adam	Adams
2. Agnes	Adverse
3. Alice	Andrews
4. Anna	Andronicus
5. Anna	Arden
6. Annabel	Bede
7. Anthony	Brand
8. Benito	Budd
9. Billy	Caesar
10. Cyrano	Cereno
11. Daisy	Cheevy

12. Daniel	Christie
13. Daniel	Clinker
14. Danny	Cory
15. Elmer	Crusoe
16. Enochde	Bergerac
17. Ethan	Deever
18. Ethan	Deronda
19. Eugene	Din
20. Eugénie	Doone
21. Forrest	Esmond
22. Gunga	Eyre
23. Hedda	Flanders
24. Henry	Frome
25. Humphrey	Gabler
26. Jane	Gantry
27. Johnny	Grandet
28. Joseph	Gray
29. Julius	Grey
30. Lolly	Gump
31. Lorna	Hudson
32. Lucy	Jones
33. Marjorie	Karenina
34. Mary	Lee
35. Miniver	Little
36. Moll	Longstocking
37. Peter	Marner
38. Pippi	Martin
39. Pudd'nhead	Miller
40. Richard	Morningstar
41. Rip	Onegin
42. Robinson	Pan
43. Roderick	Poppins
44. Roderick	Random

45. Silas	Shandy
46. Stuart	Tremaine
47. Titus	Van Winkle
48. Tom	Willowes
49. Tristram	Wilson
50. William	Wilson

Answers

1. George Eliot, *Adam Bede* 2. Anne Brontë, *Agnes Grey* 3. Booth Tarkington, *Alice Adams* 4. Leo Tolstoy, *Anna Karenina* 5. Eugene O'Neill, *Anna Christie*

6. Edgar Allan Poe, "Annabel Lee" 7. Hervey Allen, *Anthony Adverse* 8. Herman Melville, "Benito Cereno" 9. Herman Melville, *Billy Budd* 10. Edmond Rostand, *Cyrano de Bergerac*

11. Henry James, *Daisy Miller* 12. George Eliot, *Daniel Deronda* 13. John Fowles, *Daniel Martin* 14. Rudyard Kipling, "Danny Deever" 15. Sinclair Lewis, *Elmer Gantry*

16. Alfred, Lord Tennyson, "Enoch Arden" 17. Nathaniel Hawthorne, "Ethan Brand" 18. Edith Wharton, *Ethan Frome* 19. Alexander Pushkin, *Eugene Onegin* 20. Honoré de Balzac, *Eugénie Grandet*

21. Winston Groom, *Forrest Gump* 22. Rudyard Kipling, "Gunga Din" 23. Henrik Ibsen, *Hedda Gabler* 24. William Makepeace Thackeray, *Henry Esmond* 25. Tobias Smollett, *Humphrey Clinker*

26. Charlotte Brontë, *Jane Eyre* 27. Esther Forbes, *Johnny Tremaine* 28. Henry Fielding, *Joseph Andrews* 29. William Shakespeare, *Julius Caesar* 30. Sylvia Townsend Warner, *Lolly Willowes*

31. Richard Doddridge Blackmore, *Lorna Doone* 32. William Wordsworth, "Lucy Gray" 33. Herman Wouk, *Marjorie Morningstar* 34. P.L. Travers, *Mary Poppins* 35. Edwin Arlington Robinson, "Miniver Cheevy"

36. Daniel Defoe, *Moll Flanders* 37. James M. Barrie, *Peter Pan* 38. Astrid Lingren, *Pippi Longstocking* 39. Mark Twain, *Pudd'nhead Wilson* 40. Edwin Arlington Robinson, "Richard Cory"

41. Washington Irving, *Rip Van Winkle* 42. Daniel Defoe, *Robinson Crusoe*

43. Henry James, *Roderick Hudson* 44. Tobias Smollett, *Roderick Random* 45. George Eliot, *Silas Marner*

46. E.B. White, *Stuart Little* 47. William Shakespeare, *Titus Andronicus* 48. Henry Fielding, *Tom Jones* 49. Laurence Sterne, *Tristram Shandy* 50. Edgar Allan Poe, "William Wilson"

Many writers evoke just a single name in their titles. Georgette Heyer, one of the most overlooked authors of the twentieth century, did this with the likes of *Arabella, Beavallet, Helen, Sylvester,* and *Venetia,* as did Sinclair Lewis with *Arrowsmith, Babbit,* and *Dodsworth.* Identify the authors of each of these single-name titles.

1. Antigone	11. Emma	21. Nostromo
2. Brand	12. Evangeline	22. Oblomov
3. Burr	13. Frankenstein	23. Orlando
4. Camille	14. Harvey	24. Ozymandias
5. Candide	15. Herzog	25. Pamela
6. Carrie	16. Hiawatha	26. Pierre
7. Christabel	17. Ivanhoe	27. Rebecca
8. Clarissa	18. Kim	28. Sula
9. Coraline	19. Lolita	29. Tartuffe
10. Dracula	20. Nana	30. Trilby

Answers

1. Sophocles, *Antigone* 2. Henrik Ibsen, *Brand* 3. Gore Vidal, *Burr* 4. Alexandre Dumas, *Camille* 5. Voltaire, *Candide*

6. Stephen King, *Carrie* 7. Samuel Taylor Coleridge, "Christabel" 8. Samuel Richardson, *Clarissa* 9. Neil Gaiman, *Coraline* 10. Bram Stoker, *Dracula*

11. Jane Austen, *Emma* 12. Henry Wadsworth Longfellow, "Evangeline" 13. Mary Wollstonecraft Shelley, *Frankenstein* 14. Mary Ellen Chase, *Harvey* 15. Saul Bellow, *Herzog*

16. Henry Wadsworth Longfellow, "Hiawatha" 17. Walter Scott, *Ivanhoe* 18. Rudyard Kipling, *Kim* 19. Vladimir Nabokov, *Lolita* 20. Emile Zola, *Nana*

21. Joseph Conrad, *Nostromo* 23. Ivan A. Goncharov, *Oblomov* 23. Virginia Woolf, *Orlando* 24. Percy Bysshe Shelley, "Ozymandias" 25. Samuel Richardson, *Pamela*

26. Herman Melville, *Pierre* 27. Daphne du Maurier, *Rebecca* 28. Toni Morrison, *Sula* 29. Moliere, *Tartuffe* 30. George du Maurier, *Trilby*

WHOSE WHAT

The titles of many works of literature, like Lewis Carroll's *Alice's Adventures in Wonderland*, Richard Wright's *Uncle Tom's Children*, and Alan Lightman's *Einstein's Dreams*, adhere to a *possessive name + noun* pattern.

Without bobbing your Adam's apple over the prospect of opening a Pandora's Box of Achilles' heels and Hobson's choices, fill in the thirty names that kick off each title and identify the author of each work.

1. _____ 's Ashes
2. _____ 's Aunt
3. _____ 's Baby
4. _____ 's Body
5. _____ 's Cabin
6. _____ 's Castle
7. _____ 's Choice
8. _____ 's Complaint
9. _____ 's End
10. _____ 's Fan
11. _____ 's Folly
12. _____ 's Game
13. _____ 's Gift
14. _____ 's Last Case
15. _____ 's Lives

16. _____ 's Lover
17. _____ 's Mines
18. _____ 's Needle
19. _____ 's Pendulum
20. _____ 's People
21. _____ 's Pilgrimage
22. _____ 's Planet
23. _____ 's Profession
24. _____ 's Room
25. _____ 's Room
26. _____ 's Schooldays
27. _____ 's Travels
28. _____ s Wake
29. _____ 's Way
30. _____ 's Web

Answers

1. *Angela's Ashes,* Frank McCourt 2. *Charley's Aunt,* Brandon Thomas 3. *Rosemary's Baby,* Ira Levin 4. *John Brown's Body,* Stephen Vincent Benét 5. *Uncle Tom's Cabin,* Harriet Beecher Stowe

6. *Lord Weary's Castle,* Robert Lowell 7. *Sophie's Choice,* William Styron 8. *Portnoy's Complaint,* Phillip Roth 9. *Howard's End,* E.M. Forster 10. *Lady Windermere's Fan,* Oscar Wilde

11. *Almayer's Folly,* Joseph Conrad 12. *Ender's Game,* Orson Scott Card 13. *Humboldt's Gift,* Saul Bellow 14. *Trent's Last Case,* Edmund Clerihew Bentley 15. *Dubin's Lives,* Bernard Malamud

16. *Lady Chatterley's Lover,* D.H. Lawrence 17. *King Solomon's Mines,* H. Rider Haggard 18. *Gammer Gurton's Needle,* William Stevenson 19. *Foucault's Pendulum,* Umberto Eco 20. *Smiley's People,* John Le Carre

21. *Childe Harold's Pilgrimage,* Lord Byron 22. *Mr. Sammler's Planet,* Saul Bellow 23. *Mrs. Warren's Profession,* George Bernard Shaw 24. *Giovanni's Room,* James Baldwin 25. *Jacob's Room,* Virginia Woolf

26. *Tom Brown's School Days,* Thomas Hughes 27. *Gulliver's Travels,* Jonathan Swift 28. *Finnegans Wake,* James Joyce 29. *Swann's Way,* Marcel Proust 30. *Charlotte's Web,* E.B. White

THE MOTHER OF ALL TITLES

How many works have you read whose titles contain the preposition *of,* particularly the pattern *noun of a noun*? So many literary titles are cut from this fabricated cloth that the fifty in the game you are about to play are just a tiny sample.

The *noun of a noun* pattern is so formulaic that we can present each title and author as a formula. Thus, "The F of the H of U, by Edgar Allan Poe" and "The M of V, by William Shakespeare" reveal themselves as "The Fall of the House of Usher" and *The Merchant of Venice.*

The clues provided may be initially (pun intended) bewildering, but persevere and you will identify many, perhaps most, of the encrypted titles:

1. *The A of H F* by Mark Twain
2. *The A of M X* by Alex Haley
3. *The B of M C* by Robert James Waller
4. *The B of the V* by Tom Wolfe
5. "The C of A" by Edgar Allan Poe

6. *The C of the C B* by Jean Auel
7. *The C of L 49* by Thomas Pynchon
8. *The C of M C* by Alexandre Dumas
9. *The C of N T* by William Styron
10. *The C of the W* by Jack London

11. *D of a S* by Arthur Miller
12. *The D of a Y G* by Anne Frank
13. *F of F* by Erica Jong

14. *The G of W* by John Steinbeck
15. "The H of the B" by Arthur Conan Doyle

16. *The H of B A* by Frederico Garcia Lorca
17. *H of D* by Joseph Conrad
18. *The H of M* by Edith Wharton
19. *The H of N D* by Victor Hugo
20. *The H of the S G* by Nathaniel Hawthorne

21. *The I of B E* by Oscar Wilde
22. "The I of the K" by Alfred, Lord Tennyson
23. *L of the F* by William Golding
24. *L of G* by Walt Whitman
25. *The L of the M* by James Fenimore Cooper

26. *L of the R* by J.R.R. Tolkien
27. *The L of S H* by Washington Irving
28. *The M of C* by Thomas Hardy
29. *The N of the R* by Umberto Eco
30. *P of the A* by Pierre Boulle

31. *A P of the A as a Y M* by James Joyce
32. *The P of M J B* by Muriel Spark
33. *The P of T* by Pat Conroy
34. "The R of the A M" by Samuel Taylor Coleridge
35. The *R B of C* by Stephen Crane

36. The R of the L" by Alexander Pope
37. *The R of S L* by William Dean Howells
38. *R of T P* by Marcel Proust
39. *The S of B F* by W.E.B. Dubois
40. *S of F* by Katherine Anne Porter

41. *The S of K* by Ernest Hemingway
42. *The S of the L* by Thomas Harris

43. "The S L of W M" by James Thurber
44. The *S of O T* by Thornton Wilder
45. *S of S* by Toni Morrison

46. *A T of T C* by Charles Dickens
47. *T of the A* by Edgar Rice Burroughs
48. "The W of the H" by Henry Wadsworth Longfellow
49. *The W of the W* by H.G. Wells
50. *The W W of O* by L. Frank Baum

Bonus question: The T of the S by Henry James, William Shakespeare, and E.B. White. Identify all three titles.

Answers

1. *The Adventures of Huckleberry Finn* 2. *The Autobiography of Malcolm X* 3. *The Bridges of Madison County* 4. *The Bonfire of the Vanities* 5. "The Cask of Amontillado"

6. *The Clan of the Cave Bear* 7. *The Crying of Lot 49* 8. *The Count of Monte Cristo* 9. *The Confessions of Nat Turner* 10. *The Call of the Wild*

11. *Death of a Salesman* 12. *The Diary of a Young Girl* 13. *Fear of Flying* 14. *The Grapes of Wrath* 15. "The Hound of the Baskervilles"

16. *The House of Bernardo Alba* 17. *Heart of Darkness* 18. *The House of Mirth* 19. *The Hunchback of Notre Dame* 20. *The House of the Seven Gables*

21. *The Importance of Being Ernest* 22. "The Idylls of the King" 23. *Lord of the Flies* 24. *Leaves of Grass* 25. *The Last of the Mohicans*

26. *Lord of the Rings* 27. "The Legend of Sleepy Hollow" 28. *The Mayor of Casterbridge* 29. *The Name of the Rose* 30. *Planet of the Apes*

31. *A Portrait of the Artist as a Young Man* 32. *The Prime of Miss Jean Brodie* 33. *The Prince of Tides* 34. "The Rime of the Ancient Mariner" 35. *The Red Badge of Courage*

36. "The Rape of the Lock" 37. *The Rise of Silas Lapham* 38. *Remembrance of Things Past* 39. *The Souls of Black Folks* 40. *Ship of Fools*

41. "The Snows of Kilimanjaro" 42. *The Silence of the Lambs* 43. "The Secret Life of Walter Mitty" 44. *The Skin of Our Teeth* 45. *Song of Solomon*

46. *Tarzan of the Apes* 47. *A Tale of Two Cities* 48. "The Wreck of the Hesperus" 49. *The War of the Worlds* 50. *The Wonderful Wizard of Oz*

Bonus question: *The Turn of the Screw, The Taming of the Shrew,* and *The Trumpet of the Swan*

This and That

On the educational television series *The Electric Company*, children listened to this jingle:

> Conjunction Junction, what's your function?
> Hooking up words and phrases and clauses.

The conjunction *and* does indeed hook up two words in the titles of a number of literary works to make units that go together as naturally as love and marriage, hearth and home, peanut butter and jelly, and lox and bagel.

In her series of fantasy novels, mega-selling author J.K. Rowling used the small word *and* to join *Harry Potter* with *the Philosopher's Stone, the Chamber of Secrets, the Prisoner of Azkaban, the Goblet of Fire, the Order of the Phoenix, the Half-Blood Prince, the Deathly Hallows,* and *the Cursed Child.*

Make the conjunction connection by hooking each item in the first column with its titular partner in the second column. Also identify each author.

and

1. Absalom	Abel
2. Advise	Abelard
3. The Agony	Achitophel
4. Androcles	Ale
5. Angels	Anarchy

6. Antony	the Black
7. Arms	Brothers
8. The Beautiful	the Carpenter
9. The Blue	Cleopatra
10. Bread	Cleopatra
11. Cabbages	Consent
12. Caesar	Cressida
13. Cakes	the Curmudgeon
14. The Cat	the Damned
15. The Cloister	Daniel Webster
16. Crime	the Dead
17. Culture	Demons
18. Decline	Dimed
19. The Devil	the Ecstasy
20. Eleanor	the English Language
21. Fathers	Fall
22. Fire	Franklin
23. Franny	the Fury
24. Gargantua	the Glory
25. Green Eggs	Goldmund
26. Héloise	the Gray
27. Herothe	Green Knight
28. Juno	Ham
29. Kane	the Hearth
30. Man	Her Children
31. The Master	Ice
32. The Moon	Juliet
33. Mother Courage	Kings
34. The Naked	Leander
35. Narcissus	the Lion
36. Nickel	Lovers
37. Of Mice	the Man

38. Of Time	Margarita
39. The Old Man	Men
40. The Owl	Pantagruel
41. The Pitthe	Pauper
42. The Plough	the Paycock
43. Politics	Peace
44. The Power	the Pendulum
45. Pride	Prejudice
46. The Prince	Punishment
47. The Red	the Pussy-Cat
48. Romeo	Remembrance
49. Sense	the River
50. Sir Gawainthe	Rock
51. Sons	the Sea
52. The Sound	Sensibility
53. The Splendid	Sixpence
54. Strangers	Sons
55. Teathe	Stars
56. Troilus	Superman
57. The Walrus	Sympathy
58. War	The Vile
59. War	Wine
60. The Web	Zooey

Answers

1. John Dryden, *Absalom and Achitophel* 2. Allen Drury, *Advise and Consent* 3. Irving Stone, *The Agony and the Ecstasy* 4. George Bernard Shaw, *Androcles and the Lion* 5. Dan Brown, *Angels and Demons*

6. William Shakespeare, *Antony and Cleopatra* 7. George Bernard Shaw, *Arms and the Man* 8. F. Scott Fitzgerald, *The Beautiful and the Damned* 9. Bruce Catton, *The Blue and the Gray* 10. Ignazio Silone, *Bread and Wine*

11. O. Henry, *Cabbages and Kings* 12. George Bernard Shaw, *Caesar and Cleopatra* 13. W. Somserset Maugham, *Cakes and Ale* 14.

Cleveland Amory, *The Cat and the Curmudgeon* 15. Charles Reade, *The Cloister and the Hearth*

16. Fyodor Dostoevsky, *Crime and Punishment* 17. Matthew Arnold, *Culture and Anarchy* 18. Evelyn Waugh, *Decline and Fall* 19. Stephen Vincent Benét, "The Devil and Daniel Webster" 20. Joseph Lash, *Eleanor and Franklin*

21. Ivan Turgenev, *Fathers and Sons* 22. Robert Frost, "Fire and Ice" 23. J.D. Salinger, *Franny and Zooey* 24. Françoise Rabelais, *Gargantua and Pantagruel* 25. Dr. Seuss, *Green Eggs and Ham*

26. George Moore, *Héloise and Abelard* 27. Christopher Marlowe, *Hero and Leander* 28. Sean O'Casey, *Juno and the Paycock* 29. Jeffrey Archer, *Kane and Abel* 30. George Bernard Shaw, *Man and Superman*

31. Mikhael Bulgakov, *The Master and Margarita* 32. W. Somerset Maugham, *The Moon and Sixpence* 33. Bertold Brecht, *Mother Courage and Her Children* 34. Norman Mailer, *The Naked and the Dead* 35. Hermann Hesse, *Narcissus and Goldmund* 36. Barbara Ehrenreich, *Nickel and Dimed* 37. John Steinbeck, *Of Mice and Men* 38. Thomas Wolfe, *Of Time and the River* 39. Ernest Hemingway, *The Old Man and the Sea* 40. Edward Lear, "The Owl and the Pussy-Cat"

41. Edgar Allan Poe, "The Pit and the Pendulum" 42. Sean O'Casey, *The Plough and the Stars* 43. George Orwell, "Politics and the English Language" 44. Graham Greene, *The Power and the Glory* 45. Jane Austen, *Pride and Prejudice*

46. Mark Twain, *The Prince and the Pauper* 47. Stendhal, *The Red and the Black* 48. William Shakespeare, *Romeo and Juliet* 49. Jane Austen, *Sense and Sensibility* 50. the Pearl Poet, *Sir Gawain and the Green Knight*

51. D.H. Lawrence, *Sons and Lovers* 52. William Faulkner, The *Sound and the Fury* 53. C.P. Snow, *Strangers and Brothers* 54. Erik Larson, *The Splendid and the Vile* 55. Robert Anderson, *Tea and Sympathy*

56. William Shakespeare, *Troilus and Cressida* 57. Lewis Carroll, "The Walrus and the Carpenter" 58. Leo Tolstoy, *War and Peace* 59. Herman Wouk, *War and Rembrance* 60. Thomas Wolfe, *The Web and the Rock*

ROYALTIES

The first royalties were paid to kings by the commoners for the right to operate royal properties and use royal resources. Nowadays authors, like the monarchs of old, are paid royalties by publishers for the right to use their ideas and creations for profit. It's a crying shame that so few authors actually do live like kings and queens.

Who wrote these works with titles peopled by emperors and empresses and kings and queens?

1. *The Emperor Jones*
2. *The Emperor's New Clothes*
3. *Empress of the Seven Hills*
4. *Oedipus Rex*
5. *A Connecticut Yankee in King Arthur's Court*

6. *Idylls of the King*
7. *The Once and Future King*
8. *The King Must Die*
9. *King Lear*
10. *The Return of the King*

11. *King Solomon's Mines*
12. *Cabbages and Kings*
13. *Anna and the King of Siam*
14. *The Man Who Would Be a King*
15. *The Mambo Kings Play Songs of Love*

16. *The King Who Was a King*

17. *Henderson the Rain King*
18. *The Faerie Queene*
19. *Queen Mab*
20. *The Beet Queen*

21. *The African Queen*
22. *Queen*
23. *Mary Queen of Scots*
24. *The Queen of the Damned*
25. *The Black Queen*

Answers

1. Eugene O'Neill 2. Hans Christian Andersen 3. Kate Quinn 4. Sophocles 5. Mark Twain

6. Alfred, Lord Tennyson 7. T.H. White 8. Mary Renault 9 William Shakespeare 10. J.R.R. Tolkien

11. H. Rider Haggard 12. O. Henry 13. Margaret Landon 14. Rudyard Kipling 15. Oscar Hijuelos

16. H.G. Wells 17. Saul Bellow 18. Edmund Spenser 19. Percy Bysshe Shelley 20. Louise Erdrich

21. C.S. Forester 22. Alex Haley 23. Antonia Fraser 24. Anne Rice 25. Kristine Kathryn Rusch

Now, who wrote these works with titles peopled by other royal personages?

1. *The Prince*	11. *The Count of Monte Cristo*
2. *The Little Prince*	12. *The Blood Countess*
3. *The Prince and the Pauper*	13. *Lord of the Rings*
4. *The Prince of Tides*	14. *Lord of the Flies*
5. *Prince of Dogs*	15. *Lord Jim*
6. *The Princess Bride*	16. *Lord Weary's Castle*
7. *The Princess Diaries*	17. *Little Lord Fauntleroy*
8. *Princess Daisy*	18. *Lord Peter Views the Body*
9. *The Iron Duke*	19. *Lady Windermere's Fan*
10. "My Last Duchess"	20. *Lady Chatterley's Lover*

Answers

1. Niccolo Machiavelli 2. Antoine de Saint-Exupéry 3. Mark Twain 4. Pat Conroy 5. Kate Elliott

6. William Goldman 7. Meg Cabot 8. Judith Krantz 9. Meljean Brook 10. Robert Browning

11. Alexandre Dumas 12. Andre Cordrescu 13. J.R.R. Tolkien 14. William Golding 15. Joseph Conrad

16. Robert Lowell 17. Frances Hodgson Burnett 18. Dorothy L. Sayers 19. Oscar Wilde 20. D.H. Lawrence

THE BIBLE

In Their Own Words

The Bible is a book unlike any other book. It's a compilation of sixty-six books, written by more than forty authors, over a period of fifteen hundred years, on three different continents, in three different languages.

The word *bible* derives from the Greek *biblia*, which means "books." Indeed, the Bible is a whole library of books that contain many different kinds of literature—history, narrative, short stories, poetry, philosophy, riddles, fables, allegories, letters, and drama. Many parts of the Bible are highly dramatic because they show in detail the sweep of grand events as experienced by a vivid and diverse cast of persons.

In 2017, after fifty-six years representing the city where I live, the San Diego Chargers betrayed our trust and skulked away to Los Angeles. Immediately, the football team was dubbed the Los Angeles Judases. Most of us San Diego sports fans understood the biblical allusion because, reflecting the biblical story about Judas Iscariot's betrayal of Jesus, a traitorous man is now called a Judas.

As their hopes and fears, ambitions and tragedies, and laughter and sorrows unfold in the Bible, many of these men and women have become so familiar to so many readers that their names have become archetypal. Thus, a large man is a Goliath, an old man a Methuselah, a wise man a Solomon, an evil woman a Jezebel, a doer of good deeds a Good Samaritan, a long-suffering man a Job, a skeptical man a Doubting Thomas, a mighty hunter a Nimrod, and a strong man a Samson (whose luggage is Samsonite).

Many of these people reveal themselves through what they say. From their own words (as they appear in the King James Version), identify these biblical personages.

1. "The serpent beguiled me, and I did eat."
2. "Am I my brother's keeper?"
3. "After I am waxed old, shall I have pleasure, my lord being old also?"
4. "Behold the fire and the wood: but where is the lamb for a burnt offering?"
5. "Feed me, I pray thee, with that same red pottage, for I am faint."

6. "I am Esau, thy firstborn; I have done according as thou badest me: arise, I pray thee, sit and eat of my venison, that thy soul may bless me."
7. "Now therefore be not grieved, nor angry with yourselves, that ye sold me hither: for God did send me before you to preserve life."
8. "Let my people go."
9. "Take up the ark of the covenant, and let seven priests bear seven trumpets of rams; horns."
10. "O Lord God, remember me, I pray thee, and strengthen me, I pray thee, only this once, O God, that I may be at once avenged of the Philistines for my two eyes."

11. "For whither thou goest I will go; and where thou lodgest, I will lodge; thy people shall be my people and thy God my God."
12. "Behold, I have hearkened unto your voice in all ye said unto me, and have made a king over you."
13. "Am I not a Philistine, and ye servants to Saul? Choose you a man for you, and let him come down to me. If he be able to fight with me, and to kill me, then will we be your servants."
14. "Why have ye conspired against me, thou and the son of Jesse?"

15. "Thou art the man. Thus saith the Lord God of Israel, I anointed thee king over Israel, and I delivered thee out of the hand of Saul."

16. "O my son Absalom! My son, my son Absalom! Would God I had died for thee, O Absalom, my son, my son!"

17. "Divide the living child in two, and give half to the one, and half to the other."

18. "If it please the king, and if I have found favor in his sight, and the thing seem right before the king, and I be pleasing in his eyes, let it be written to reverse the letters devised by Haman the son of Hammedatha the Agagite, which he wrote to destroy the Jews which are in all the king's provinces."

19. "Naked came I out of my mother's womb, and naked shall I return thither: the Lord gave, and the Lord hath taken away; blessed be the name of the Lord."

20. "Curse God, and die."

21. "One basket had very good figs, even like the figs that are first ripe: and the other basket had very naughty figs, which could not be eaten, they were so bad."

22. "My God hath sent his angel, and hath shut the lions' mouths, that they have not hurt me."

23. "Take me up, and cast me forth into the sea; so shall the sea be calm unto you: for I know that for my sake this great tempest is upon you."

24. "Go and search diligently for the young child; and when ye have found him, bring me word again, that I may come and worship him also."

25. "I indeed baptize you with water unto repentance; but he that cometh after me is mightier than I."

26. "I do not know the man."

27. "I have sinned in that I have betrayed the innocent blood."

28. "My God, my God, why hast thou forsaken me?"

29. "Take ye him, and crucify him: for I find no fault in him."

30. "Though I speak with the tongues of men and of angels, and have not charity, I am become as sounding brass, or a tinkling cymbal."

Answers

1. Eve. Genesis 3:13
2. Cain. Genesis 4:9
3. Sarah. Genesis 18:12
4. Isaac. Genesis 22:7
5. Esau. Genesis 25:30

6. Jacob (not Esau). Genesis 27:19
7. Joseph. Genesis 45:5
8. Moses. Exodus 5:1
9. Joshua. Joshua 6:6
10. Samson. Judges 16:28

11. Ruth. Ruth 1:16
12. Samuel. I Samuel 12:1
13. Goliath. I Samuel 17:8-9
14. Saul. I Samuel 22:13
15. Nathan. II Samuel 12:7

16. David. II Samuel 18:33
17. Solomon. I Kings 3:25
18. Esther. Esther 8:5
19. Job. Job 1:21
20. Job's wife. Job 2:9

21. Jeremiah. Jeremiah 24:2
22. Daniel. Daniel 6:22
23. Jonah. Jonah 1:12

24. Herod. Matthew 2:8
25. John the Baptist. Matthew 3:11

26. Peter. Matthew 26:72
27. Judas. Matthew 27:4
28. Jesus. Mark 15:34
29. Pontius Pilate. John 19:6
30. Paul. I Corinthians 13:1

Bible by the Numbers

"In a hundred years the Bible will be a forgotten book found only in museums," predicted French author Voltaire, writing from his home in Geneva. A century later his home was owned and occupied by the Geneva Bible Society.

The Bible is also the best-selling book of all time. *The Guinness Book of World Records* estimates that more than five billion copies have been sold or distributed. In fact, if all the books ever printed were gathered into one great pile, the majority would be bibles.

The thirty-nine books of the Old Testament, the twenty-seven books of the New Testament, and the fifteen books of the Apocrypha compose the Bible. Translated into more than two thousand languages, the Bible is available to about eighty percent of the world's people. Each year in the United States alone, approximately twenty million copies are purchased and many more copies given away.

With those vital statistics in mind, try your hand and memory at playing a biblical numbers game.

1. How many books of the Bible compose the Hebrew torah?
2. How many books of the Bible are named after women?
3. How many days did it take God to create the world?
4. How many times are the words *apple* and *snake* mentioned in the King James Bible version of Genesis? What about the word *whale* in Jonah?
5. How many rivers were in Eden?

6. How long did Methuselah live?

7. How many cubits in length did God command Noah to build the ark?

8. How many of each animal went onto the ark?

9. How many people were saved on the ark?

10. How long did the flood last?

11. God agreed to spare Sodom and Gomorrah if Abraham could find how many righteous people there?

12. How old was Abraham when his son Isaac was born?

13. How many patriarchs were there?

14. How many brothers did Joseph have?

15. How many kine were in the dream that Pharaoh related to Joseph?

16. How many tribes of Israel were there?

17. How many plagues were visited on the Egyptians because Pharaoh would not let the people of Israel go?

18. How many years did Israel wander in the desert?

19. How many commandments did God deliver to Moses on Mount Sinai?

20. How many times did Balaam smite his ass?

21. How many days did Joshua and his army circle Jericho, blowing their trumpets at its walls?

22. How many men did Samson slay with the jawbone of an ass?

23. How long did Solomon rule over Israel?

24. How many wives and how many concubines did Solomon have?

25. How long did Jonah remain in the belly of the fish?

26. How many comforters did Job have?

27. According to the Psalms, how many years are allotted to each human being?

28. Which psalm begins "The Lord is my shepherd; I shall not want. He maketh me to lie down in green pastures"?

29. How many beasts did Daniel dream of?

30. How many friends of Daniel did God save from the fiery furnace?

Answers

1. The first five books of the Bible—Genesis, Exodus, Leviticus, Numbers, and Deuteronomy

2. Two in the Old Testament—Ruth and Esther; two in the Apocrypha—Judith and Susanna.

3. Six. Genesis 1:31

4. Zero for all three. *Fruit, serpent,* and *great fish* occur a number of times. 5. Four. Genesis 2:10

6. 969 years. Genesis 5:27

7. Three hundred. Genesis 6:15

8. Two. Genesis 7:14-16. But note Genesis 7:2-3, which numbers the clean beasts and fowls of the air by sevens

9. Eight. Noah, his wife, their three sons, and their wives. Genesis 6:18.

10. Forty days. Genesis 7:17. But note "And the waters prevailed upon the earth a hundred and fifty days." Genesis 7:24

11. Ten. Genesis 18:32

12. One hundred years old. Genesis 21:5

13. Three: Abraham, Isaac, and Jacob.

14. Eleven. Genesis 35:22

15. Fourteen: seven fat and seven lean. Genesis 41:17-20.

16. Twelve. Genesis 49:28

17. Ten. Exodus 7:1-12:33

18. Forty. Joshua 5:6

19. Ten. Exodus 20:3-17

20. Three. Numbers 22:28

21. Seven. Joshua 6:14-15

22. A thousand. Judges 15:15
23. Forty years. I Kings 11:42
24. Seven hundred and three hundred. I Kings 11:3
25. Three days and nights. Jonah 1:17

26. Three: Eliphaz, Bildad, and Zophar. Job 2:11
27. Seventy. Psalms 90:10
28. The twenty-third.
29. Four. Daniel 7:3-7
30. Three: Shadrach, Meshach, and Abednego. Daniel 3:19

Now crunch each number in the New Testament.

1. The New Testament contains how many gospels?
2. How many months older than Jesus was John the Baptist?
3. How many apostles did Jesus recruit?
4. How many miracles did Jesus perform? Thirty-seven.
5. How many days did Jesus fast in the desert?

6. How many parables did Jesus tell?
7. How many men did Jesus feed with how many loaves and how many fishes?
8. How many people passed by the injured man who had fallen among thieves before the Samaritan stopped to help?
9. In the parable of the vineyard workers, at what hour were the last ones hired?
10. For how many days had Lazarus lain dead before being raised by Jesus?

11. In Jesus's parable of the virgins, how many virgins were there? How many were wise and how many foolish?
12. By the end of the parable of the talents, how many talents had the man who had originally been given five?
13. How many Beatitudes did Jesus deliver?
14. With how many thieves was Jesus crucified?

15. How many pieces of silver did Judas Iscariot receive for his betrayal of Jesus?

16. How many hours did Jesus hang on the cross before he died?
17. How many times did Peter deny Jesus?
18. How many times did Jesus foretell his own death?
19. How many times was Jesus whipped on the way to the cross?
20. How many Marys told of Jesus's resurrection?

21. How many days occurred between Jesus's death and his resurrection?
22. How many epistles of Paul appear in the Bible?
23. The Book of Revelation mentions a scroll closed with how many seals?
24. How many Horsemen of the Apocalypse were there?
25. What is the Number of the Beast?

Answers
1. Four: Matthew, Mark, Luke, and John
2. Six. Luke 1:26
3. Twelve. Matthew 10:2
4. Thirty-seven.
5. Forty. Matthew 4:2

6. Believe it or not, sixty-four.
7. Five thousand, with five loaves and two fishes. Mark 6:38 and 6:44, Luke 9:13-14, John 6:9-10
8. Two, a priest and a Levite. Luke 10:31-32
9. The "eleventh hour." Matthew 20:6
10. Four. John 11:17

11. Ten: five wise and five foolish. Matthew 25:1-2
12. Eleven. Matthew 25:28
13. Nine. Matthew 5:3-11

14. Two. Mark 15:27

15. Thirty. Matthew 26:15, 27:3

16. Six. Mark 15:25 and 15:34

17. Three. Matthew 20: 17-19, Mark 10:32-34, and Luke 18:31-34

18. Three. Matthew 26:69-75

19. Thirty-nine. The figure is never specified in the Bible, but thirty-nine is the traditional number of lashes that the Romans administered.

20. Two: Mary Magdalene and Mary the mother of James. Luke 24:10

21. Three. Matthew 27:63

22. Fourteen: Roman, Corinthians I and II, Galatians, Ephesians, Philippians, Colossians, Thessalonians I and II, Timothy I and II, Philemon, Hebrews, and James.

23. Seven. Revelation 5:1 and 8:1

24. Four. Revelation 6:2-8

25. 666. Revelation 13:18

BIBLE RIDDLES

Riddles are perhaps the most ancient of all verbal puzzles, dating back at least twenty-five hundred years. In the book of Judges, the mighty Samson comes upon a swarm of bees making honey in the carcass of a lion. From this, Samson makes a bet with the Philistines that they cannot solve his riddle: "Out of the eater came something to eat. Out of the strong came something sweet." After seven days of weeping, Samson's wife wheedles the answer out of him and conveys it to the Philistines. In a rage, Samson kills thirty of them and lays waste their city. Today we don't take riddles quite as seriously, but we do derive sweetness and strength from a cleverly turned poser.

Why were Adam and Eve the happiest couple in history?
Because Eve couldn't tell Adam how many other men she could have married, and Adam couldn't tell Eve how much he loved his mother's cooking.

Why were Adam and Eve kicked out of the Garden of Eden?
Because they were the first to ignore Apple terms & conditions.

What excuse did Adam give to his children as to why he no longer lived in Eden? "
Your mother ate us out of house and home."

Also from the Book of Genesis: Joe the Gorilla at the zoo was very smart. The man in charge of Joe's care asked the ape, "Can I bring you some books to read?"

Joe said, "Yes. Please bring me a Bible and a book by Charles Darwin."

"Why do you want to read those books?" asked the employee.

Joe answered, "I want to know if I'm my brother's keeper or my keeper's brother."

How was baseball played throughout the Bible?

In the big inning, Eve stole first. Adam balked but stole second. Cain struck out Abel. During the great flood, humanity was rained out. Gideon rattled the pitchers. Saul was put out by David. Absalom and Judas went out swinging. And the prodigal son stole home.

The Bible has inspired not only an outpouring of great literature, art, and music, but also an impressive array of riddles based on its stories. The canon of biblical riddles reminds us that we can laugh as well as be inspired by and learn from with the Bible.

1. What did God say right after he created twenty-four hours of light and darkness?

2. What animals disobeyed God's command to be fruitful and multiply?

3. Who was the champion runner of all time?

4. What was the longest day in the Bible?

5. At what time of day was Adam created?

6. Why couldn't Eve have measles?

7. Did Eve ever have a date with Adam?

8. On what did the earliest people do arithmetic lessons?

9. How were Adam and Eve prevented from gambling?

10. What did Adam and Eve never have but left to their children?

11. What evidence is there that Adam and Eve were pretty noisy?

12. How long did Cain hate his brother?

13. When was meat first mentioned in the Bible?

14. What animal took the most baggage into the ark; what animals took the least?

15. Why weren't there any worms in the ark?

16. What creatures were not on the ark?

17. Where did Noah keep the bees?

18. Who were the best financiers in the Bible?

19. Where did all the people in the world hear one rooster crow?

20. Why couldn't people play cards on the ark?

21. Where was Noah when the lights went out?

22. Why couldn't Noah catch many fish?

23. When is paper money first mentioned in the Bible?

24. What did the cat say when the ark landed?

25. Why was Lot's wife turned into a pillar of salt?

26. When was tennis first played in the Bible?

27. Who was the first man in the Bible to use a computer?

28. How does Moses make his coffee?

29. What did the Egyptians do when it got dark?

30. Who was the first man in the Bible to break all Ten Commandments?

31. How do we know for certain that Moses was a male?

32. Who were the three most constipated men in the Bible?

33. Who was the greatest actor in the Bible? What did he die of?

34. What kind of a man was Boaz before he got married?

35. How was Ruth rude to Boaz?

36. Why was Goliath astonished when David hit him with a stone?

37. Who was older, David or Goliath?

38. Why was the prophet Elijah like a horse?

39. Who was the most successful doctor in the Bible?
40. What did Job have to cover his sackcloth and ashes?

41. Who was the strongest man in the Bible?
42. Who was Jonah's guardian?
43. How is the story of Jonah an inspiration?
44. How was John the Baptist like a penny?
45. Who were the three tiniest apostles?

46. Who set the record for the high jump in the Bible?
47. What kind of cars can be found in the Bible?
48. How could Jesus enjoy a glass of wine anytime he wanted it?
49. Why was Princess Salome the greatest jockey of all time?
50. What three noblemen are mentioned in the Bible?

Answers

1. "I'm going to call it a day." 2. adders 3. Adam. He was first in the human race. 4. The one with no Eve. 5. A little before Eve.

6. Because she'd Adam. 7. No, it was an apple. 8. God told them to multiply on the face of the earth. 9. They lost their paradise. 10. belly buttons.

11. They raised Cain. 12. As long as he was Abel. 13. When Noah took Ham into the ark. 14. The elephant took his trunk, but the fox and the rooster took only a brush and comb between them. 15. Because worms come in apples, not in pairs.

16. Fish. 17. In the ark hives. 18. Noah, who floated his stock while the whole world was in liquidation, and Pharaoh's daughter, who took a little prophet from the rushes on the banks. 19. In the ark. 20. Noah sat on the deck.

21. In d'ark. 22. He only had two worms. 23. When the dove brought the green back to the ark. 24. Is that Ararat? 25. Because she was dissatisfied with her Lot.

26. When Joseph served in Pharaoh's court. 27. Moses. He downloaded data from the cloud to his tablet. 28. Hebrews it. 29. They turned on the Israelites. 30. Moses.

31. He wandered around the desert for forty years and never stopped to ask for directions. 32. Cain, because he wasn't Abel; Methuselah, who sat on the throne for 900 years; and Moses, because God gave him two tablets and sent him into the wilderness. 33. Samson. He brought down the house, then died of fallen arches. 34. Ruthless. 35. She pulled his ears and stepped on his corn.

36. It had never entered his head before. 37. David. He rocked Goliath to sleep. 38. He was fed from aloft. 39. Job. He had the most patience. 40. Three miserable comforters.

41. Jonah. The whale couldn't keep him down. 42. The whale brought him up. 43. Jonah was down in the mouth but came out all right. 44. He was one sent. 45. Peter, James, and John. They all slept on a watch.

46. Jesus, when he cleared the temple. 47. Jehovah drove Adam and Eve out of the Garden in a Fury. David's Triumph was heard throughout the land. And the apostles were all in one Accord. 48. All he had to do was start with a glass of water. 49. She got a head of John the Baptist on a charger. 50. Barren Fig Tree, Lord How Long, and Count Thy Blessings.

NAME THAT TUNE!

From the riddles in the preceding chapter, it's clear that the Bible is so baked into our culture that joke after joke stands on the shoulders of its content. Here's a playlist of theme songs. Match each biblical character with his or her appropriate popular song. *Examples:* Shadrach, Meshach, and Abednego's song would be "Great Balls of Fire!" owing to their placement into a fiery furnace by Nebuchadnezzar II in the Book of Daniel. Conversely, Eliphaz, Bildad, and Zophar's, who advised a blameless Job to repent, would be paired with "Cold Comfort."

1. Absalom	"Blinded By the Light"
2. Adam and Eve	"Coat of Many Colors"
3. Bathsheba	"Crying Over You"
4. Cain	"Do It Now, Do It Good"
5. Daniel	"Hair"
6. David	"I Could Have Danced All Night"
7. Esther	"I Feel Pretty"
8. The Good Samaritan	"I Got You Babe"
9. Jezebel	"I'm Sorry"
10. Job	"The Lady Is a Tramp"
11. John the Baptist	"Let's Hear It For the Boy"
12. Jonah	"The Lion Sleeps Tonight"
13. Joseph	"Losing My Head Over You"
14. Lazarus	"Psycho Killer"

15. The Magi	"Raindrops Keep Fallin' on My Head"
16. Mary Magdalene	"Rebel, Rebel"
17. Methuselah	"The Second Time Around"
18. Moses	"Shadow of a Doubt"
19. Noah	"Starry Starry Night"
20. Paul	"Stayin' Alive"
21. Peter	"Strangers in Paradise"
22. Pharaoh's daughter	"The Wanderer"
23. Salome	"A Whale Of a Tale"
24. Samson	"Why's Everybody Always Picking on Me?"
25. Thomas	"Your Cheatin' Heart"

Answers

1. Absalom: "Rebel, Rebel" 2. Adam and Eve: "Strangers in Paradise" 3. Bathsheba: "Your Cheatin' Heart" 4. Cain: "Psycho Killer" 5. Daniel: "The Lion Sleeps Tonight"

6. David: "Let's Hear It For the Boy" 7. Esther: "I Feel Pretty" 8. The Good Samaritan: "Do It Now, Do It Good" 9. Jezebel: "The Lady is a Tramp" 10. Job: "Why's Everybody Always Picking on Me?"

11. John the Baptist: "Losing My Head Over You" 12. Jonah: "A Whale Of a Tale" 13. Joseph: "Coat of Many Colors" 14. Lazarus: "The Second Time Around" 15. The Magi: "Starry Starry Night"

16. Mary Magdalene: "Crying Over You" 17. Methuselah: "Stayin' Alive" 18. Moses: "The Wanderer" 19. Noah: "Raindrops Keep Fallin' on My Head" 20. Paul: "Blinded By the Light"

21. Peter: "I'm Sorry" 22. Pharaoh's daughter: "I Got You Babe" 23. Salome: "I Could Have Danced All Night" 24. Samson: "Hair" (could also be Absalom) 25. Thomas: "Shadow of a Doubt"

Good Words
From the Good
Book

A front-page story in a St. Louis newspaper reported an incident in which two men were hospitalized after a fistfight. A car had stopped for a red light at a main intersection. A man on the sidewalk called out to its driver, "Hey, Mister, your left front tire is going flat." The driver got out, looked at the tire, and called to his benefactor, "Thanks for being a good Samaritan!" Whereupon the pedestrian leaped off the curb and started pounding the driver with his fists, shouting, "You can't call me a dirty name!" The shocked driver struck back, and the result was that both men ended up in the hospital—all because one of them thought that being identified as a "Samaritan" was insulting.

Few of us will end up eating a knuckle sandwich because we miss the source of a biblical allusion. In this case it's Luke 10:30-37, about a Samaritan who rescued a man who had fallen among thieves and been left half dead. Our lives are considerably enriched when we are able to identify such sources, because allusions become keys that unlock the doors to many mansions—itself a biblical reference to John 14:2, where Jesus says, "In my Father's house are many mansions."

While the spiritual values of the Bible are almost universally recognized, the enduring effect of the Bible on the English language is often overlooked. The fact is, though, that a great number of biblical words, references, and expressions have become part of our everyday speech, so that even people who don't read the Bible carry its text on their tongues.

163

Identify the biblically inspired words described below:

1. In ancient times, a _____ was a unit of weight, and this weight of silver or gold constituted a monetary unit, one that figures prominently in a parable of Jesus: "For the kingdom of heaven is as a man travelling into a far country, who called his own servants, and delivered unto them his goods. And unto one he gave five _____, to another two, and to another one; to every man according to his several ability." (Matthew 25:14-15)

The most common modern meaning of the word _____, some special, often God-given ability or aptitude, is a figurative development from the parable.

2. An obstacle: "Thou shalt not curse the deaf, nor put a _____ before the blind, but shalt fear thy God." (Leviticus 19:14)

3. A special celebration: "And ye shall hallow the fiftieth year, and proclaim liberty throughout all the land unto all the inhabitants thereof: it shall be a _____ unto you." (Leviticus 25:10)

4. "Now when Jesus was risen early the first day of the week, he appeared first to Mary Magdalene, out of whom he had cast seven devils. And she went and told them that had been with him, as they mourned and wept." (Mark 16:9-10) Mary Magdalene became a favorite subject of medieval and Renaissance painters, who traditionally depicted her as weeping. The tearful Mary was portrayed so sentimentally that, over the years, her name has been transformed into the word _____, which has come to mean "tearfully sentimental."

5. A final, decisive battle, marked by overwhelming slaughter: "And he gathered them together into a place called in the Hebrew tongue _____ ... And there were voices, and thunders, and lightnings; and there was a great earthquake, such as was not since men were upon the earth, so mighty an earthquake, and so great." (Revelation 16:16, 18)

6. Anything of enormous size: "Behold now _____, which I made with thee ... Behold, he drinketh up a river and hasteth not: he trusteth that he can draw up Jordan into his mouth." (Job 40:15, 23).

7. Anything of enormous size: "In that day the Lord with his sore and great and strong sword shall punish _____ the piercing serpent, even _____ that crooked serpent; and he shall slay the dragon that is in the sea." (Isaiah 27:1)

8. "How doth the city sit solitary that was full of people! How is she become as a widow! She that was great among the nations, and princess among the provinces, how is she become tributary!" (Lamentations 1.1)

That passage is a typically dark passage in one of the prophetic books, from which we derive the word _____, meaning a sorrowful tirade, extended lament, or bitter denunciation.

9. "Then the Lord of the _____ gathered them together for to offer a great sacrifice unto Dagon their god, and to rejoice." (Judges 16:23)

Because the nation described above were an alien, non-Semitic people who worshiped strange gods, their name became a term for a foreigner. Nineteenth-century philosophers, such as Thomas Carlyle and Matthew Arnold, further changed the meaning of the word so that today _____ is a derogatory term for one who shuns intellectual and cultural activities.

10. In Judges 12:5-6, we learn about a conflict between the peoples of Gilead and Ephraim: "And the Gileadites took the passages of Jordan before the Ephraimites; and it was so, that when those Ephraimites which were escaped said, Let me go over; that the men of Gilead said unto him, Art thou an Ephraimite? If he said, Nay; then they said unto him, Say now _____" (Judges 12:5-6).

Because the *sh* sound didn't occur in the language of the Ephraimites, they couldn't pronounce the word correctly, and forty-two thousand of them were slain. That's how the word has acquired the meaning that it has today: a password, catchword, or slogan that distinguishes one group from the other.

Answers

1. talent 2. stumbling block 3. jubilee 4. maudlin 5. armageddon
6. behemoth 7. leviathan 8. jeremiad 9. philistine 10. shibboleth

HOLY MOSES!

A long with the works of William Shakespeare, the King James Bible is the most fruitful source of everyday phrases in the English-speaking world. Exclamations like "Holy Moses!" and "Judas Priest!" are the most obvious, but a profusion of other biblical phrases season our speech.

Many such expressions are direct borrowings, such as "kingdom come," in Matthew 6:10, and "the eleventh hour," from Matthew's version of Jesus's parable of the workers in the vineyard who gained employment so late in the day (Matthew 20:6).

Others have entered our modern idiom in a slightly revised form, as "crystal clear" (from "clear as crystal" in Revelation 22:1) and "by the skin of my teeth." The latter echoes Job's lament in Job 19:20: "My bone cleaveth to my skin and to my flesh, and I am escaped with the skin of my teeth" ("*by* the skin of my teeth" in the Revised Standard Version). "But teeth don't have any skin," you protest. In the biblical phrase, the "skin" refers to a margin of safety as thin as the enamel on the teeth.

In the Song of Solomon 7:4, the beloved is told, "Thy neck is as a tower of ivory." From this comparison derives the modern cliché "an ivory tower," which picks up the sense of beauty, loftiness, and unassailability implied by the original words.

Still other expressions are general references to a biblical story, like "Adam's apple," so called because many men, but few women, exhibit a bulge of laryngeal cartilage in front of their throats. According to male-dominated folklore, Eve swallowed her apple without care or residue, while a chunk of the fruit stuck in the throat of the innocent and misled Adam.

Here, listed in the order they occur in the Bible, are fifty biblical turns of phrase that have survived the centuries pretty much unscathed. Complete each item:

1. Saw the _____ (Genesis 1:4)
2. My brother's _____ (Genesis 4:9)
3. Sold his _____ for a mess of _____ (Genesis 25:33-34)
4. The _____ of the land (Genesis 45:18)
5. A land flowing with _____ and _____ (Exodus 3:17)

6. Man doth not live by _____ alone (Deuteronomy 8:3)
7. The _____ of his eye (Deuteronomy 32:10)
8. A hair's _____ (Judges 20:16)
9. A man after his own _____ (I Samuel 13:14)
10. Played the _____ (I Samuel 26:21)

11. A still small _____ (I Kings 19:12)
12. Weeping and _____ (Esther 4:3)
13. Give up the _____ (Job 3:11)
14. In the land of the _____ (Job 28:13)
15. Out of the mouths of _____ (Psalms 8:2)

16. His heart's _____ (Psalms 10:3)
17. At their wit's _____ (Psalms 107:27)
18. Labor in _____ (Psalms 127:1)
19. Out of the _____ (Psalms 130:1)
20. Pride goeth ... before a _____ (Proverbs 16:18)

21. Vanity of _____ (Ecclesiastes 1:2)
22. There is nothing new under the _____ (Ecclesiastes 1:9)
23. Eat, drink, and be _____ (Ecclesiastes 8:15)
24. As white as _____ (Isaiah 1:18)
25. They shall beat their _____ into _____ (Isaiah 2:4)

26. Woe is _____! (Isaiah 6:5)
27. See eye to _____ (Isaiah 52:8)
28. Holier than _____ (Isaiah 65:5)
29. Weighed in the _____ (Daniel 5:27)
30. Salt of the _____ (Matthew 5:13)

31. Good for _____ (Matthew 5:13)
32. An eye for an _____, and a tooth for a _____ (Matthew 5:38)
33. Pearls before _____ (Matthew 7:6)
34. House _____ against itself (Matthew 12:25)
35. Fell by the _____ (Matthew 13:4)

36. Signs of the _____ (Matthew 16:3)
37. A den of _____ (Matthew 21:13)
38. Blood _____ (Matthew 27:6)
39. In his right _____ (Mark 5:15)
40. Physician, _____ thyself (Luke 4:23)

41. A law unto _____ (Romans 2:14)
42. The powers that _____ (Romans 13:1)
43. It is high _____ (Romans 13:11)
44. In the twinkling of an _____ (I Corinthians 15:52)
45. A _____ in the flesh (II Corinthians 12:7)

46. Labor of _____ (I Thessalonians 1:3)
47. The root of all _____ (I Timothy 6:10)
48. Keep the _____ (II Timothy 4:7)
49. Cover a _____ of sins (I Peter 4:8)
50. Bottomless _____ (Revelation 9:1, 20:1)

Answers

1. light 2. keeper 3. birthright, pottage 4. fat 5. milk / honey
6. bread 7. apple 8. breadth 9. heart 10. fool
11. voice 12. wailing 13. ghost 14. living 15. babes
16. desire 17. end 18. vain 19. depths 20. fall
21. vanities 22. sun 23. merry 24. snow 25. swords / plowshares
26. me 27. eye 28. thou 29. balances 30. earth
31. nothing 32. eye, tooth 33. swine 34. divided 35. wayside
36. times 37. thieves 38. money 39. mind 40. heal
41. themselves 42. be 43. time 44. eye 45. thorn
46. love 47. evil 48. faith 49. multitude 50. pit

The Bible in the News

The steed bit his master.
How came that to pass?
He heard the good pastor
Say, "All flesh is grass."

In this anonymous ditty, the horse chomps his master because of two errors of judgment. The misguided equine takes too literally the metaphor "All flesh is grass" and fails to recognize that the pastor was making an allusion, in this case to Isaiah: 40:6-7: "All flesh is grass, and all goodness thereof, is as the flower of the field: The grass withereth, the flower fadeth: because the spirit of the Lord bloweth upon it: surely the people is grass."

Houses of worship are not the only vessels filled with biblical allusions. Because the Bible occupies such a central place in our culture, news stories employ biblical references to make their points concisely and powerfully. Identify the biblical element in each of the modern stories that follow.

1. Someone possessing the patience of Job explained to Senator Sanders the unsustainable trajectory of entitlement programs.
2. Believe me, I want my kids back in school as much as the next parent, but the writing is on the wall. And it seems we might be wise to read it and to act accordingly rather than pursuing a fantasy of packed lunch bags and morning rushes to the school bus stop.

3. Mike Pompeo, an evangelical Christian who keeps an open Bible by his desk, now says it's possible that God raised up Donald Trump as a modern Queen Esther.

4. Referring to the Houston Astros' stealing signs from the Los Angeles Dodgers in the 2017 World Series: The first baseball player to steal a sign was Noah, who was tipped that fastball weather was on its way.

5. In Russia, hyperinflation, the worst scourge of all, threatens like some angry Goliath.

6. For everything there is a season, including one for "coming out," the custom whereby young women are presented to that privileged class called "society."

7. Now, without being quite ready to lie down like the lion with the lamb, these business and labor leaders say they want to work together for the national interest.

8. COMPUTER PEOPLE ARE CREATING A VALLEY OF BABBLE IN CALIFORNIA (headline about Silicon Valley).

9. From any human perspective, a terrorist attack aboard an airplane was horrible. But the terrorists didn't win either. Whether that's worth it in terms of deterrence, discouraging future terrorists, that takes a Solomon-like judgment.

10. The only thing you need to be a successful farmer these days is faith, hope, and parity.

Answers

1. In the Old Testament book bearing his name, Job, an upright and wealthy man, endures a series of awful tragedies but refuses to curse God.

2. Daniel, chapter 5, tells the story of the spectral fingers of a man's hand writing a message on the wall for King Belshazzar. The prophet Daniel interpreted the message to mean "Thou art weighed in the balances and art found wanting."

3. In the Book of Esther, Esther, a Jewish woman, became the wife of the Persian king Ahasuerus. She interceded successfully with the king on behalf of her people.

4. The story of Noah and the flood as told in Genesis 6:9-8:11 .

5. In I Samuel 17:4-54, the young shepherd David slays the supposedly invincible giant Goliath with his slingshot.

6. In Ecclesiastes 3:1, we learn that "To everything there is a season, and a time to every purpose under the heaven."

7. Isaiah 11:6 paints a scene in which "The wolf shall dwell with the lamb, and the leopard shall lie down with the kid, and the calf and the young lion and the fatling together."

8. In Genesis 11:1-9, we learn of a Tower of Babel that was built to reach unto heaven. God scotches the project by fragmenting the language of the builders into many tongues.

9. King Solomon was noted for the wisdom of his judgment, the most famous of which, as told in I Kings 3:16-28, was a decision between two women who both claimed to be the mother of one infant. 10. A clever pun on Paul's famous advice in I Corinthians 13:13: "And now abideth faith, hope, and charity, these three; but the greatest of these is charity."

MYTHOLOGY

TEST YOUR MYTHOLOGY IQ

Legend has it that Alexander the Great always carried a treasured copy of Homer's *Iliad* and that he put it under his pillow at night, along with his sword. When Alexander defeated the Persian king Darius III, a golden casket studded with gems was among the booty. Inside that chest Alexander placed his edition of Homer, proclaiming, "There is but one thing in life worthy of so precious a casket." Classical mythology is itself a golden and bejeweled casket of literature, philosophy, and religion.

> Knock, knock.
> Who's there?
> Electrolux.
> Electrolux who?
> Electrolux her father, but not her mother.

You would have to possess a high mythological IQ to understand the humor of that little knock-knock joke, which is based on a reader's knowledge of Aeschylus's *Oresteia*. When Agamemnon, king of Greece, returned from the Trojan War, his wife Clytemnestra murdered him in his bath. Their daughter, Electra, who remained loyal to her father, sought a fatal revenge against her mother.

Knowledge of ancient Greek mythology helps you to understand a phalanx of riddles and jokes. For example, what mythological monster always had a bad-hair day? The answer is Medusa, a Gorgon monster whose hairdo consisted of live venomous snakes. For another example, Yo momma so ugly she turns Medusa into stone. Turns out that anyone who looked at Medusa's face turned to stone. And if that person was a musician, he or she instantly became a rock star.

Allusions like these allow us to experience an idea on two levels at once by linking what we are reading or hearing with what we have read or heard in the past. Allusions enhance the present through experiences that glow through time. Our lives are enriched when we are able to identify such references because allusions play an important role in creating impressions and emotions.

To see how powerful your mythological literacy is, I've prepared a test of Olympian proportions. The world of classical mythology is essentially a human world. Realizing how splendid men and women could be, the Greeks and Romans made their gods and goddesses in their own images.

Match the items in columns two and three with each god and goddess in column one.

Greek name	Latin name	Realm
1. Aphrodite	Ceres	agriculture
2. Ares	Diana	fire and the forge
3. Artemis	Dis	hearth and home
4. Bacchus/ Dionysus	Faunus	king of gods and men
5. Demeter	Juno	love and beauty
6. Hades/Pluto	Jupiter/Jove	messenger of gods
7. Hephaestus	Liber	moon and the hunt
8. Hera	Mars	nature
9. Hermes	Mercury	queen of gods
10. Hestia	Minerva	sea
11. Pallas Athena	Neptune	sun
12. Pan	Phoebus Apollo	underworld
13. Phoebus Apollo	Venus	war
14. Poseidon	Vesta	wine and revelry
15. Zeus	Vulcan	wisdom

Answers

1. Aphrodite / Venus, love and beauty 2. Ares / Mars, war 3. Artemis / Diana, moon and the hunt 4. Bacchus/Dionysus / Liber, wine and revelry 5. Demeter /Ceres, agriculture

6. Hades/Pluto / Dis, underworld 7. Hephaestus / Vulcan, fire and the forge 8. Hera / Juno, queen of gods 9. Hermes / Mercury, messenger of gods 10. Hestia / Vesta, hearth and home

11. Pallas Athena / Minerva, wisdom 12. Pan / Faunus, nature 13. Phoebus Apollo/ Phoebus Apollo (same name in Greek and Latin), sun 14. Poseidon / Neptune, sea 15. Zeus / Jupiter/Jove, king of gods and men

Now you are invited to hit a Homer. The following characters are all involved in the epic events of the Trojan War, chronicled in Homer's *Iliad* and other ancient works.

Match each name in the first column with the appropriate description in the second.

1. Achilles — best friend of Achilles
2. Agamemnon — chief warrior for the Greeks
3. Andromache — daughter of Agamemnon
4. Astyanax — the face that launched a thousand ships
5. Ajax — feigned madness to avoid the war

6. Cassandra — greatest Trojan warrior
7. Diomedes — husband of Helen
8. Hector — judge of a beauty contest
9. Hecuba — king of Troy
10. Helen — leader of Greek forces

11. Iphigenia — loud-voiced herald
12. Laocoön — mother of Achilles
13. Menelaus — oldest and wisest of the Greeks
14. Nestor — prophetess to whom no one listened

15. Odysseus	queen of Troy
16. Paris	second greatest Greek warrior
17. Patroclus	son of Hector
18. Priam	warned Trojans of Trojan horse
19. Stentor	went mad
20. Thetis	wife of Hector

Answers

1. chief warrior for the Greeks 2. leader of Greek forces 3. wife of Hector 4. son of Hector 5. went mad

6. prophetess to whom no one listened 7. second greatest Greek warrior 8. greatest Trojan warrior 9. queen of Troy 10. the face that launched a thousand ships

11. daughter of Agamemnon 12. warned Trojans of Trojan horse 13. husband of Helen 14. oldest and wisest of the Greeks 15. feigned madness to avoid the war

16. judge of a beauty contest 17. best friend of Achilles 18. king of Troy 19. loud-voiced herald 20. mother of Achilles

You odyssey this quiz. The following characters live in Homer's *Odyssey*.

Match each name in the first column with the appropriate description in the second.

1. Antinous	arrogant suitor
2. Argus	beautiful, dangerous witch
3. Calypso	fatal singer
4. Circe	hero of the Odyssey
5. Odysseus	nymph who loved Odysseus
6. Penelope	Odysseus's dog
7. Scylla	sea monster
8. Siren	son of Odysseus

9. Telemachus   Theban prophet
10. Tiresias   wife of Odysseus

Answers

1. arrogant suitor 2. Odysseus's dog 3. nymph who loved Odysseus 4. beautiful, dangerous witch 5. hero of the *Odyssey*

6. wife of Odysseus 7. sea monster 8. fatal singer 9. son of Odysseus 10. Theban prophet

THERE'S A GOD IN YOUR SENTENCE

Mythology is one of the richest literary sources that flow into our English language. The ancient gods, goddesses, heroes, and heroines are not dead. We who are alive today constantly speak, hear, write, and read their names, even if we don't always know it.

The word *echo*, for example, is an echo of a story that is three millennia old. Echo was a beautiful nymph who once upon a time aided Zeus in a love affair by keeping his wife, Hera, occupied in conversation. As a punishment for such verbal meddling, Hera confiscated Echo's power to initiate conversation and allowed her to repeat only the last words of anything she heard.

Such was a sorry enough fate, but later Echo fell madly in love with an exceedingly handsome demigod, Narcissus, who, because of Echo's peculiar handicap, would have nothing to do with her. So deeply did the nymph grieve for her unrequited love that she wasted away until nothing was left but her voice, always repeating the last words she heard.

The fate that befell Narcissus explains why his name has been transformed into words like *narcissism* and *narcissistic*, pertaining to extreme self-love. One day Narcissus looked into a still forest lake and beheld his own face for the first time, although he did not know it was his. He at once fell in love with the beautiful image, and he, like Echo, pined away for a love that could never be consummated.

Using the following descriptions, identify the gods and goddesses, heroes and heroines, and fabulous creatures that inhabit the world of classical mythology and the words that echo them.

1. One of the vilest of mythological villains was a king who cooked and served the body of his young son Pelops to the gods. They soon discovered the king's wicked offering, restored the dead boy to life, and devised a punishment to fit the crime. They banished the king to Hades, where he is condemned to stand in a sparkling pool of water with boughs of luscious fruit overhead; when he stoops to drink, the water drains away through the bottom of the pool, and when he wishes to eat, the branches of fruit sway just out of his grasp. Ever since, then something presents itself temptingly to our view, we invoke this king's name.

2. An adjective that means "merry, inspiring mirth" comes from the name the ancient Romans gave to the king of their gods because it was a happy omen to be born under his influence.

3. The frenetic Greek nature god was said to cause sudden fear by darting out from behind bushes and frightening passers-by. That fear now bears his name.

4. The goddess of love and beauty gives us several words from both her Greek and Roman names.

5. A Greek herald in Homer's *Iliad* was a human public address system, for his voice could be heard all over camp. Today, the adjective form of his name means "loud-voiced, bellowing."

6. The most famous of all of Homer's creations spent ten years after the fall of Troy wandering through the ancient world encountering sorceresses and Cyclopes. The wily hero's name lives on in the word we use to describe a long journey or voyage marked by bizarre turns of events.

7. Nine daughters of Zeus were the personification of the arts, including dance, theater, poetry, and musical instruments.

8. Another great Greek hero needed all his power to complete twelve exceedingly laborious labors. We use a form of his name to describe a mighty effort or an extraordinarily difficult task.

9. A tribe of female warriors cut off their right breasts in order to handle their bows more efficiently. The name of their tribe originally meant "breastless"; it now means "a strong woman."

10. Because of its fluidity and mobility, quicksilver is identified by a more common label that is the Roman name for Hermes, the winged messenger of the gods. That name has also bequeathed us an adjective meaning "swift, eloquent, volatile."

Answers

1. Tantalus-tantalize 2. Jove-jovial 3. Pan-panic 4. Aphrodite-aphrodisiac, hermaphrodite; Venus-venereal, venerate 5. Stentor-stentorian

6. Odysseus-odyssey 7. the muses-music, museum 8. Hercules-herculean 9. Amazons-amazon 10. Mercury-mercury, mercurial

MYTHIC RIDDLES

I don't know much about Greek mythology. It's my Achilles elbow. But I do know enough to lay some mythological riddles on you. The most famous riddle of all is the one that the Sphinx put to Oedipus: "What goes on four legs in the morning, on two at noon and on three at night?" Oedipus, one of the first game-show contestants, answered: "Man. In infancy, he crawls. In his prime, he walks. In old age, he leans on a staff." He was correct and thus became Oedipus Rex.

As a more modern riddle asks: What's the difference between a centaur and a senator?

Answer: One is half man and half horse's ass—and the other is a creature in mythology.

Clearly the joke works best if, from your knowledge of Greek mythology, you are able to conjure an image of a centaur—equine in the nether regions but with the head, arms, and torso of a human being.

What is a Cyclops's favorite song?

Answer: "I Only Have Eye for You."

The punchline is most effective if you know that the Cyclopes sported only one eye (and thus had 20 vision).

Please take a minotaur two to provide the answers to as many mythic riddles as you can about the Greek gods, goddesses, and gyros.

1. Summarize Greek mythology in five words.
2. What is the main drain on Zeus's bank account?
3. What does Zeus wear under his clothes?
4. What did Zeus say to Athena when she sprang from his head in full armor?
5. What do you call the goddess of knowledge when she has no friends?

6. What Greek figure started a new kind of music?
7. Why doesn't Aphrodite date tennis players?
8. What Greek god can referee a tennis match without having to turn back and forth?
9. In Greek mythology, who are the angriest goddesses?
10. What is Medusa's favorite cheese?

11. Why would Prometheus be a good mailman?
12. What carry-out meal is evil?
13. Why did the town stop issuing parking tickets when Persephone was carried off to the underworld?
14. Why did the Cyclops couple get along so well?
15. What games did the children of the Greek gods play?

16. What do Greeks use to sculpt statues of their mythological gods and heroes?
17. How do Greek women get ready for a toga party?
18. What kind of horse was the Trojan horse?
19. Which Greek hero was in need of a podiatrist?
20. What do Achilles and an honest politician have in common?

Answers

1. "Unfortunately, Zeus was feeling horny." 2. Child support. 3. Thunderwear. 4. "Girl, you are really getting on Minerva." 5. Pal-less Athena.

6. Sisyphus. He was the first rock and roller. 7. Because love means nothing to them. 8. Janus. He has two faces that look in opposite directions. 9. The three Furies. 10. Gorgonzola.

11. Because it's a job that involves a lot of de-livering. 12. Pandora's box lunch. 13. Demeter wasn't working. 14. They saw eye to eye on everything. 15. Hydra go seek and pick up Styx.

16. Con-Crete. 17. With a Hera pointment. 18. A phony pony that turned into a night mare. 19. Achilles. He was weak in the heel. 20. They're both imaginary people.

NAME THAT TUNE!

Match each mythological figure with the appropriate popular song. For example, the theme song for Electra would be "My Heart Belongs to Daddy," for Hephaestus "If I Had a Hammer," and for the Amazons "I Hate Men."

1. Achilles	"All You Need Is Love"
2. Agamemnon	"Bottle of Wine"
3. Ajax	"Come Fly With Me"
4. Aphrodite	"Crazy"
5. Apollo	"Fly Me to the Moon"
6. Artemis	"Goldfinger"
7. Atlas	"Greased Lightning"
8. Cerberus	"Hello Darkness, My Old Friend"
9. Circe	"Here Comes the Sun"
10. Dionysus	"Hey Good Lookin'"
11. Echo	"King of the Road"
12. Hades	"Light My Fire"
13. Helen of Troy	"Looking For Love In All the Wrong Places"
14. Hercules	"Master of the Sea"
15. Icarus	"Put a Spell on You"
16. King Midas	"Red Hot Mama"
17. Medusa	"Rock Around the Clock"
18. Mercury	"Say It Loud"
19. Narcissus	"Speed Racer"

20. Odysseus	"Stand By Your Man"
21. Oedipus	"Stronger"
22. Pan	"Turn to Stone"
23. Pegasus	"The Wanderer"
24. Penelope	"The Warrior"
25. Poseidon	"Weight of the World"
26. Prometheus	"Who Let the Dogs Out?"
27. Sisyphus	"Wild Horses"
28. Stentor	"Wild Thing"
29. Tantalus	"You Can't Always Get What You Want"
30. Zeus	"You're So Vain"

Answers

1. Achilles: "The Warrior" 2. Agamemnon, "King of the Road"
3. Ajax: "Crazy" 4. Aphrodite: "All You Need Is Love" 5. Apollo: "Here Comes the Sun"

6. Artemis "Fly Me to the Moon" 7. Atlas: "Weight of the World" 8. Cerberus: "Who Let the Dogs Out?" 9. Circe: "Put a Spell on You" 10. Dionysus: "Bottle of Wine" 11. Echo: "Looking for Love In All the Wrong Places" 12. Hades: "Hello Darkness My Old Friend" 13. Helen of Troy (also Narcissus): "Hey Good Lookin'" 14. Hercules: "Stronger" 15. Icarus: "Come Fly With Me"

16. King Midas: "Goldfinger" 17. Medusa: "Turn To Stone" 18. Mercury: "Speed Racer" 19. Narcissus: "You're So Vain" 20. Odysseus: "The Wanderer"

21. Oedipus: "Red Hot Mama" 22. Pan: "Wild Thing" 23. Pegasus: "Wild Horses" 24. Penelope: "Stand By Your Man" 25. Poseidon: "Master of the Sea"

26. Prometheus: "Light My Fire" 27. Sisyphus: "Rock Around the Clock" 28. Stentor: "Say It Loud" 29. Tantalus: "You Can't Always Get What You Want" 30. Zeus: "Greased Lightning"

MYTHIC HEADLINES

KING KILLS HIS FATHER, THEN MARRIES WOMAN
OLD ENOUGH TO BE HIS MOTHER—AND SHE IS!

This banner statement describes the story of Oedipus, who, as things turned out, married the girl just like the girl that married dear old dad. That is, he blindly got hitched to his own mother, Jocasta.

Now identify ten more ancient tales from these often lurid modern-day headlines:

1. COURT UPHOLDS SUIT AGAINST
   CHIEF GOD FOR CHILD SUPPORT

2. GREEK MERCENARY DONE IN
   BY ARROW IN HIS HEEL

3. QUEEN MURDERS KING IN HIS BATH

4. WILY HUSBAND SLAUGHTERS
   PARTY GUESTS HITTING ON HIS WIFE

5. WICKED WITCH TURNS MEN INTO PIGS

6. CRAZY STRONGMAN MURDERS OWN KIDS
   LATER CHOPS OFF MONSTER'S HEADS

7. FIERY GOD PUNISHED EACH DAY
    BY EAGLE EATING HIS LIVER

8. ATHENIAN PRINCE'S
    A-MAZE-ING FEAT:
    SLAYS FEROCIOUS BULL

9. MUSICAL GENIUS DECIDES TO GO
    TO HELL TO SAVE MAIN SQUEEZE

10. GREEK GOD LAPS FIELD IN 100-YARD DASH

Answers

1. Unfaithful Zeus conducted frequent dalliances with mortal women that produced many children.

2. In the *Iliad*, Paris shot an arrow into Achilles' heel, fatally wounding him.

3. In the *Orestia*, Queen Clytemnestra murdered her husband, King Agamemnon, in his bath.

4. In the *Odyssey*, Odysseus returned home to Ithaca and slew Penelope's suitors. 5. In the *Odyssey*, the witch Circe turned men swine.

6. Heracles (Hercules to the Romans) was driven mad by Hera and killed his wife and children. Later, he multiply beheaded the Lernaean Hydra.

7. The gods punished Prometheus by sending the Caucasian Eagle to devour his liver, which grew back each day.

8. The monster Medusa's hairdo consisted of living venomous snakes.

9. Orpheus descended into Hades to rescue his love, Eurydice.

10. The god Mercury wore winged sandals, which endowed him with super speed.

MYTHOLOGY IN THE NEWS

Whizzing around the internet is this tongue-in-cheek virus warning:

Hey, Hector,

This was forwarded to me by Cassandra—it looks legit. Please distribute to Priam, Hecuba, and your Trojan citizens. Thanks, Laocoön

WARNING! WARNING! WARNING!

If you receive a gift in the shape of a large wooden horse, do not download it! It is extremely destructive and will overwrite your entire city!

The "gift" is disguised as a large wooden horse about two stories tall. It will show up outside the city gates and appear to be abandoned. Do not let it through the gates! It contains hardware that is incompatible with Trojan programming, including a crowd of heavily armed Greek warriors who will destroy your army, sack your town, and kill your women and children. If you have already received such a gift, do not open it! Take it out of the city unopened and set fire to it by the beach.

Forward this message to everyone you know!

This extended satirical allusion is to the decade-long Trojan War, chronicled in Homer's epic, *The Iliad*. Priam and Hecuba were king and queen of Troy and their son Hector its bravest defender.

In an effort to win the war, the Greeks sent a huge wooden horse to the Trojans as an offering to Athena. A host of soldiers were hiding inside the horse. The priest Laocoön warned the Trojans to beware of Greeks bearing gifts but was crushed by two giant serpents. That night, the Greek soldiers emerged from the horse and overthrew Troy.

Classical mythology is far from dead. It's alive and well and living in our newspapers and magazines and on the internet.

Identify the mythic characters and creatures echoed in each of the news stories below.

1. Evidently, AIDS viruses can sequester themselves inside macrophages soon after infection and before antibodies are made. The microphage acts as a Trojan Horse for AIDS viruses, hiding and even transporting them around the body.

2. In the absence of more aggressive federal efforts to keep these vaping devices off the market, parents and teachers are left with the Sisyphean task of trying to keep them out of children's hands.

3. When the soccer gods decided to make the national soccer team invincible, they dipped the team into the river by its goalkeeper, the beleaguered Claudio Taffarel—their one weak link, their lone concession to mortality.

4. We do not generally execute highly placed political figures in part because that opens up a Pandora's Box that may expose American officials to assassination.

5. There's an opportunity here for a group to rise out of the ashes and continue on with the mission that was the Women's March.

6. We surely felt we couldn't build those luxury boxes with the sword of Damocles hanging over our heads.

7. This fear of technological progress—and the anxieties that accompany it— starting with the Greek poet Hesiod, who described how humans "dwelt in ease and peace upon their lands" before

Prometheus and his new technology (fire stolen from Zeus) ruined everything.

8. At the same time, a variety of baby-girl dolls were born like Athena from the head of Zeus—or the head of the toy corporation.

9. The Daedalus project began with the goal of designing, building and testing a human-powered aircraft that could fly the mythical distance, 115 km. To achieve this goal, three aircraft were constructed. The Light Eagle was the prototype aircraft, weighing 92 pounds. On January 22, 1987, it set a closed course distance record of 59 km, which still stands.

10. For thirty years, the Boston Celtics were the best—and luck-iest—team in the NBA. Now it's all turned around. They've lost their Midas touch.

Answers

1. The allusion in this statement appears in the introduction to this chapter.

2. In classical mythology, Sisyphus is condemned to eternal punishment in the underworld, where he rolls a massive rock up a slope, only to have it roll back down just as he reaches the top.

3. Achilles, the hero of the Trojan War, was dipped in the river Styx by his mother, the nymph Thetis, to make him immortal. But she held him by his heel, and his heel did not get wet. Ultimately, Hector shot a fatal arrow into Achilles' heel.

4. Pandora ("woman of all gifts") was the first human woman, an ancient Greek Eve. She opened a jar (a box in the popular mind), and out flew a myriad of plagues and evils.

5. The phoenix was a long-lived bird that could be regenerated or reborn by rising from the ashes of its predecessor.

6. Damocles was a courtier whose king, Dionysius of Syracuse, allowed him to sit on the throne for a single day. But above that throne hung a heavy sword suspended by a single horsehair. After just one day of high anxiety, Damocles begged Dionysius to return to sitting on the throne.

7. The Titan Prometheus stole fire from the gods and gave it to humanity.

8. The goddess Athena is said have sprung fully formed and fully armored from the head of her father, Zeus.

9. Daedalus built two pairs of colossal wings of wax and feathers to escape King Minos. His son Icarus and he put on the wings; but as they flew away from Crete, the boy soared upward, too close to the sun. Icarus's wings melted, and he plunged into the sea and drowned.

10. Everything King Midas touched turned to gold.

SHAKESPEARE

Brush Up Your Shakespeare

As the Huntsman in *King Henry VI* says, "This way, my lord, for this way lies the game." Here's an untrivial quiz on a far-from-trivial author. Supply the basic facts about William Shakespeare's life and works that the following twenty questions ask for.

1. Identify the years of Shakespeare's birth and death. For extra credit, identify the month and day.

2. In what town and country was Shakespeare born?

3. Name the monarchs who reigned in Shakespeare's country during his lifetime.

4. Name Shakespeare's wife. No, you don't get points for "Mrs. Shakespeare."

5. How many children did the Shakespeares have?

6. With what theater was Shakespeare most intimately connected?

7. What was the name of Shakespeare's acting company?

8. Where were these lines first published?:

> Good frend for Jesus sake forbeare,
> To digg the dust encloased heare!
> Blest be ye man yt spares thes stones,
> And curst be he yt moves my bones.

9. One of Shakespeare's contemporaries rightly foresaw the magnitude of the Bard's achievement when he wrote of Shakespeare: "He was not of an age, but for all time!" Name the writer of that sentence.

10. How many plays did Shakespeare write?

11. What are the three categories by which the plays are generally classified?

12. Into how many acts is each play traditionally divided?

13. In what verse form did Shakespeare write his plays?

14. What do we call the first edition of Shakespeare's collected works?

15. Some scholars believe that Shakespeare didn't write Shakespeare. Name three of the top six (out of the more than eighty) candidates who supposedly ghostwrote for the Bard.

16. How many sonnets are in Shakespeare's sonnet sequence?

17. How many lines are in a Shakespearean sonnet?

18. In what poetic meter are the sonnets written?

19. Identify the Shakespeare plays begun by each of the following lines:

    a. Two households, both alike in dignity,
       In fair Verona, where we lay our scene,
       From ancient grudge break to new mutiny,
       Where civil blood makes civil hands unclean.

    b. Hence! home, you idle creatures, get you home!
       Is this a holiday?

    c. If music be the food of love, play on

    d. Who's there?

    e. When shall we three meet again?
       In thunder, lightning, or in rain?

20. Name the Shakespearean heroes with whom each of the following enemies contends: *a.* Iago *b.* Macduff *c.* Laertes and

Claudius *d.* Hotspur *e.* Octavius Caesar *f.* Richmond *g.* Brutus and Cassius.

As Belarius exclaims in *Cymbeline*, "The game is up!" It's now time to consult the answers.

Answers

1. and 2. Shakespeare was baptized in Holy Trinity Church in the English village of Stratford-upon-Avon on April 26, 1564, and probably entered the earthly stage three days earlier. He exited his life's play in Stratford on April 23, 1616.

3. Elizabeth I and James I.

4. Anne Hathaway.

5. Three: Susanna and the twins Hamnet and Judith.

6. The Globe.

7. For most of his career, Shakespeare was a member of the Lord Chamberlain's Company, later known as the King's Men.

8. These words are the epitaph on Shakespeare's grave in the chancel of the Holy Trinity Church.

9. Ben Jonson.

10. Thirty-seven.

11. Tragedies, comedies, and histories.

12. Five.

13. blank verse: unrhymed iambic pentameter.

14. the First Folio

15. The ever-shifting slate of candidates includes Walter Raleigh; Edward de Vere, seventh Earl of Oxford; William Stanley, sixth Earl of Derby Francis Bacon; Christopher Marlowe; and Mary Herbert, Countess of Pembroke.

16. 154.

17. fourteen.

18. Iambic pentameter, as in the plays.

19. *a. Romeo and Juliet b. Julius Caesar c. Twelfth Night d. Hamlet e. Macbeth.*

20. *a.* Othello *b.* Macbeth *c.* Hamlet *d.* Prince Hal (later Henry V) *e.* Antony *f.* Richard III *g.* Julius Caesar.

RAISING THE BARD

Now that you've taken a fairly straightforward quiz about William Shakespeare, prepare yourself for some trick questions. Because these posers are fraught with snares, delusions, and arcane knowledge, don't expect to get many of them right. Still, you'll find that the answers will make fascinating reading:

1. What do the following sentences have in common?:

> We all make his praise.
> I swear he's like a lamp.
> "Has Will a peer?" I ask me.
> Ah, I speak a swell rime.
> Wise male. Ah, I sparkle!
> Hear me, as I will speak.
> I'll make a wise phrase.
> I'm a weakish speller.

2. How do Shakespeare's birth and death days relate to St. George and Miguel de Cervantes?

3. Who is the Merchant of Venice?

4. In the famous balcony scene in *Romeo and Juliet*, Juliet says, "O Romeo, Romeo! wherefore art thou Romeo?" What does *wherefore* mean?

5. How many times does the word *witch* appear in the dialogue of *Macbeth*?

6. When Cleopatra's lover asked her if she was in love with him, she answered, "Oh, Marc, I am!" Whether or not you caught my pun on "Omar Khayyam," correctly spell Marc's last name.

7. What character speaks the greatest number of lines in Shakespeare's plays?

8. What play contains the greatest number of Shakespearean lines? What play contains the smallest number?

9. What do these Shakespearean plays have in common?: *Love's Labor's Lost, The Taming of the Shrew, A Midsummer Night's Dream,* and *Hamlet.*

10. What do Hamlet's father, Banquo, and Julius Caesar have in common?

11. What do these Shakespearean plays have in common?: *The Merchant of Venice, As You Like It, Twelfth Night,* and *Cymbeline.*

12. "All the world's a stage … and one man in his _____ plays many parts." Provide the missing word. In what play does this famous speech appear? Explain how in the same play a male plays a female who plays a male who plays a female.

13. So you think you know your Shakespeare and can quote his lines with exquisite accuracy? Examine these six Shakespearean quotations and provide the missing words:

a. "Alas, poor Yorick! I knew him _____" *(Hamlet)*
b. "To _____ the lily" *(King John)*
c. "All that _____ is not gold" *(The Merchant of Venice)*
d. "_____ will have his day" *(Hamlet)*
e. "To the _____ born" *(Hamlet)*
f. "We are such stuff as dreams are made _____" *(The Tempest)*

14. Are Shakespeare's sonnets addressed to a man or a woman?

15. What do the following words have in common?: *auspicious, bedroom, critic, dwindle, frugal, generous, majestic, obscene, submerge.*

Answers

1. Each of these sentences is an anagram of *William Shakespeare,* and each uses all the letters in his name.

2. Shakespeare was almost certainly born on April 23—Saint George's Day—in 1564, and he died on the same day fifty-two years later, the same day on which the Spanish writer Miguel de Cervantes expired.

3. Antonio, not Shylock.

4. "Why," not "where." The spoken stress should be placed on *Romeo,* not *art.*

5. Only twice, I, 3, 6: "Aroint thee, witch!" and IV, 1, 23: "witch's mummy." While the word *witch* appears many times in the stage directions, the lines of the play generally refer to the witches as "weird sisters."

6. Antony, not Anthony.

7. With a total of 1,422 lines, an actor playing Hamlet has more to learn than anyone playing any other single part in a single play by Shakespeare. But the character who speaks the greatest number of lines in Shakespeare is Sir John Falstaff—1,178 in *Henry IV,* Parts I and II, and an additional 436 lines in *The Merry Wives of Windsor,* for a total of 1,614 lines.

8. *Hamlet,* with 3,931 lines, is the longest of Shakespeare's plays, and *The Comedy of Errors,* with 1,778, is the shortest. But the answer to the question of what play contains the smallest number of Shakespearean lines is not *The Comedy of Errors.* That's because Shakespeare collaborated with other playwrights on *Henry VIII* (to which he contributed 1,167 lines), *Pericles* (1,140 lines), and *The Two Noble Kinsmen,* which he wrote with John Fletcher and to which he contributed 1,131 lines.

9. Each play contains a play within a play.

10. Hamlet's father, Banquo, and Julius Caesar are three of Shakespeare's personages who return as ghosts.

11. Each play involves a woman who disguises herself as a man.

12. *Time*, not *life*. Most people say Hamlet, but it is Jaques who delivers this speech in *As You Like It* (Act II, scene 7). In the earliest productions of Shakespeare's plays, only men and boys were allowed into the theater companies. In *As You Like It*, a male played the part of Rosalind, who, in the story, flees to the Forest of Arden disguised as a young man, who then pretends to be a woman in order to help her paramour, Orlando, practice his wooing.

13. *a. Horatio*, not *well;*
    b. paint, not *gild;*
    c. glisters, not *glitters;*
    d. dog, not *every dog;*
    e. manner, not *manor*
    f. on, not *of.*

14. Both. Most are addressed to a young man, but twenty-eight of the one-hundred-fifty-four sonnets are addressed to or about a woman.

15. They are among the more than seventeen hundred words invented by Shakespeare, who, "bethumpt with words," *(King John)* was truly "a man of fire-new words" *(Love's Labor's Lost)*.

IN THEIR OWN WORDS

William Shakespeare's plays, which he wrote in London between approximately 1590 and 1613, have been in almost constant production since their creation. Because the playwright dealt with universal truths and conflicts in human nature, his tragedies, comedies, and history plays continue to draw audiences from all walks of life, just as they did more than four centuries ago.

Shakespeare's tragedies, comedies, and histories are the most performed ever, in large part because of their vivid and oh-so-human beings. From some of the best-known lines shot from the Bardic canon, identify these Shakespeare characters and the plays in which he (or she) "struts and frets his hour upon the stage":

1. "To be, or not to be: that is the question."
2. "What's in a name? That which we call a rose
   By any other name would smell as sweet."
3. "Is this a dagger which I see before me,
   The handle toward my hand?"
4. "Friends, Romans, countrymen. Lend me your ears."
5. "How sharper than a serpents tooth it is to have a thankless child."

6. "We are such stuff
   As dreams are made on, and our little life
   Is rounded with a sleep."
7. "The quality of mercy is not strained.
   It droppeth as the gentle rain from heaven
   Upon the place beneath."

8. "Then must you speak
    Of one who loved not wisely but too well."
9. "Oh brave new world that has such people on it."
10. " Some are born great, some achieve greatness, and some have greatness thrust upon them."

11. "If you prick us, do we not bleed? If you tickle us, do we not laugh? If you poison us, do we not die? And if you wrong us, shall we not revenge?"
12. "Beware the Ides of March."
13. "If music be the food of love, play on."
14. "To thine own self be true,
    And it shall follow as the night to day,
    Thou canst not be false to any man."
15. "The better part of valor is discretion."

16. "The course of true love never did run smooth."
17. "A horse! a horse! my kingdom for a horse!"
18. "All that glisters is not gold."
19. "Lord, what fools these mortals be!"
20. "Uneasy lies the head that wears the crown."

21. "But, for mine own part, it was Greek to me."
22. "This royal throne of kings, this sceptered isle…
    This blessed plot, this earth, this realm, this England."
23. "I will wear my heart upon my sleeve
    For daws to peck at."
24. "All the world's a stage,
    And all the men and woman merely players.
    They have their exits and their entrances,
    And one man in his time plays many parts."
25. "My words fly up, my thoughts remain below:
    Words without thoughts never to heaven go."

26. "Out, damned spot. Out, I say!"

27. "A plague on both your houses!"
28. "Cowards die many times before their deaths. The valiant never taste of death but once."
29. "Sweets to the sweet."
30. "Give me my robe, put on my crown. I have Immortal longings in me."

Answers

1. Hamlet, *Hamlet* III, 1, 58
2. Juliet, *Romeo and Juliet*, II, 2, 91-92
3. Macbeth, *Macbeth*, II, 1, 33-34
4. Marc Antony, *Julius Caesar*, III, 2, 77
5. King Lear, *King Lear*, I, 4, 288-289

6. Prospero, *The Tempest*, IV, 1, 156-158
7. Portia, *The Merchant of Venice*, IV, 1, 181-183
8. Othello, *Othello*, V, 2, 344-345
9. Miranda, *The Tempest*, V, 1, 183-184
10. Malvolio, *Twelfth Night*, II, 5, 156-159

11. Shylock, *The Merchant of Venice*, III, 1, 61-63
12. the soothsayer, *Julius Caesar*, I, 2, 20
13. Duke Orsino, *Twelfth Night*, I, 1, 1
14. Polonius, *Hamlet*, I, 3, 120-122
15. Falstaff, *Henry IV, Part I*, V,4, 120-121

16. Lysander, *A Midsummer Night's Dream*, I, 1, 134
17. Richard III, *Richard III*, V, 4, 7
18. message in the gold casket, *The Merchant of Venice*, II, 7
19. Puck, *A Midsummer Night's Dream*, III, 2, 115
20. Henry IV, *Henry IV, Part 2*, III, 1, 31

21. Casca, *Julius Caesar*, I, 2, 280
22. John of Gaunt, *Richard II*, II, 1, 40 and 50
23. Iago, *Othello*, I, 1, 64

24. Jaques, *As You Like It*, II, 7, 139-2
25. Claudius, *Hamlet*, III, 3, 100-101

26. Lady Macbeth, *Macbeth*, V, I, 36
27. Mercutio, *Romeo and Juliet*, III, 1, 91
28. Julius Caesar, *Julius Caesar*, II, 2, 32-33
29. Gertrude, *Hamlet*, V, 1, 243
30. Cleopatra, *Antony and Cleopatra*, V, 2, 282-283

A MAN OF MANY TITLES

William Shakespeare was a busy and prolific writer who, in twenty-five years, turned out thirty-seven plays and co-authored several others. His loving labors provide a rich source of titles for their books to generations of authors who return again and again to the well of his felicitous phrasing.

Take *Macbeth*. Near the end of the play, Macbeth expresses his darkening vision of life: "It is a tale/Told by an idiot, full of sound and fury,/Signifying nothing." Centuries later, William Faulkner purloined a phrase from that speech for his novel *The Sound and the Fury*, which is indeed told by an idiot, Benjy Compson. Earlier in the play one of the witches chants, "By the pricking of my thumbs,/ Something wicked this way comes." Agatha Christie plucked the first line and Ray Bradbury the second as titles of their bestsellers.

Other progeny from just the one play *Macbeth* include Robert Frost's "Out, Out," Rose Macaulay's *Told by an Idiot*, Adrienne Rich's *Of Woman Born*, Ngaio Marsh's *Light Thickens*, Anne Sexton's *All My Pretty Ones*, Alistair MacLean's *The Way to Dusty Death*, Ruth Rendell's *To Fear a Painted Devil*, Robert B. Parker's *All Our Yesterdays*, Terry Pratchett's *Wyrd Sisters*, Philip Barry's *Tomorrow and Tomorrow*, Malcolm Evans's *Signifying Nothing*, and John Steinbeck's *The Moon is Down*.

Clearly, William Shakespeare was one of the most generous souls who ever set quill to parchment. Although he himself was never granted a title, he freely granted titles to others. Identify the literary titles plucked from the following lines.

RICHARD LEDERER

1. O brave new world that has such people in't!
–THE TEMPEST, V, 1, 183

2. The ears are senseless that should give us hearing,
   To tell him his commandment is fulfill'd,
   That Rosencrantz and Guildenstern are dead.
   Where should we have our thanks?
–HAMLET, V, 2, 369

3. Now is the winter of our discontent
   Made glorious summer by the son of York;
   And all the clouds that low'rd upon our house
   In the deep bosom of the ocean buried.
-RICHARD III, I, 1, 1

4. There are no tricks in plain and simple faith;
   But hollow men, like horses hot at hand,
   Make gallant show and promise of their mettle;
-JULIUS CAESAR, IV, 2, 22-24

5. Art thou any more than a steward? Dost thou think because
   thou art virtuous there will be no more cakes and ale?
-TWELFTH NIGHT, II, 3, 114-115

6. When to the sessions of sweet silent thought
   I summon up remembrances of things past,
   I sigh the lack of many a thing I sought,
   And with old woes new wail my dear time's waste;
-SONNET XXX, 1-4

7. And Caesar's spirit, ranging for revenge,
   With Ate by his side come hot from hell,
   Shall in these confines with a monarch's voice
   Cry 'Havoc,' and let slip the dogs of war,
-JULIUS CAESAR, III, 1, 270-273

210

8. The sun's a thief, and with his great attraction
   Robs the vast sea; the moon's an arrant thief,
   And her pale fire she snatches from the sun;
-TIMON OF ATHENS, IV, 3, 436-438

9. What may this mean,
   That thou, dead corse, again in complete steel,
   Revisits thus the glimpses of the moon;
-HAMLET, I, 4, 51-152

10. Men at some time are masters of their fates;
    The fault, dear Brutus, is not in our stars,
    But in ourselves, that we are underlings.
-JULIUS CAESAR, 1, 2, 139-141

Answers

1. Aldous Huxley, *Brave New World* 2. Tom Stoppard, *Rosencrantz and Guildenstern are Dead* 3. John Steinbeck, *The Winter of Our Discontent* 4. T.S. Eliot, "The Hollow Men" 5. W. Somerset Maugham, *Cakes and Ale*

6. Marcel Proust, *Remembrance of Things Past* 7. *Cry Havoc*, John Hamilton Lewis, and Frederick Forsyth, *The Dogs of War* 8. Vladimir Nabokov, *Pale Fire* 9. Edith Wharton, *The Glimpses of the Moon* 10. James M. Barrie, *Dear Brutus,* and John Green, *The Fault in Our Stars*

NOT A PASSING PHRASE

Oscar Wilde once quipped, "Now we sit through Shakespeare in order to recognize the quotations." Unrivaled in so many other ways in matters verbal, Shakespeare is unequaled as a phrasemaker. "All for one, one for all," and "not a creature was stirring—not even a mouse," wrote Alexandre Dumas in *The Three Musketeers* and Clement Clark Moore in *A Visit From St. Nicholas*. But Shakespeare said them first—"One for all, or all for one we gage" in *The Rape of Lucrece* and "not a mouse stirring" in *Hamlet*.

A student who attended a performance of *Hamlet* came away complaining that the play was "nothing more than a bunch of clichés." The reason for this common reaction is that so many of the memorable expressions in *Hamlet* have become proverbial. In that one play alone were born *brevity is the soul of wit; there's the rub; to thine own self be true; it smells to heaven; the very witching time of night; the primrose path; though this be madness, yet there is method in't; dog will have his day; the apparel oft proclaims the man; neither a borrower nor a lender be; frailty, thy name is woman; something is rotten in the state of Denmark; more honored in the breach than the observance; hoist with his own petard; the lady doth protest too much; to be, or not to be; sweets to the sweet; to the manner born; in my heart of hearts; yeoman's service;* and *more in sorrow than in anger*.

Cudgel thy brains to complete these expressions that first saw the light in the other plays of William Shakespeare:

1. all the world's a _____ (*As You Like It*, II, 7, 139)
2. as good _____ would have it (*The Merry Wives of Windsor*, III, 5, 72)
3. the better part of valor is _____ (*Henry IV, Part 1*, V, 4, 120)
4. a blinking _____ (*The Merchant of Venice*, II, 9, 54)
5. break the _____ (*The Taming of the Shrew*, I, 2, 262)

6. breathed his _____ (*Henry VI, Part 3*, V, 2, 40)
7. come full _____ (*King Lear*, V, 3, 174)
8. the course of true love never did run _____ (*A Midsummer Night's Dream*, I, 1, 134)
9. eaten me out of house and _____ (*Henry IV, Part 2*, II, 1, 67)
10. every _____ a king (*King Lear*, IV, 6, 107)

11. for _____ sake (*Henry VIII*, Prologue, 23)
12. a foregone _____ (*Othello*, III, 3, 428)
13. the green-eyed _____ (*Othello*, III, 3, 166)
14. have seen better _____ (*As You Like It*, II, 7, 120)
15. household _____ (*Henry V*, IV, 3, 52)

16. if music be the food of love, _____ (*Twelfth Night*, I, 1, 1)
17. infinite _____ (*Antony and Cleopatra*, II, 2, 236)
18. an itching _____ (*Julius Caesar*, IV, 3, 10)
19. laid on with a _____ (*As You Like It*, I, 2, 94)
20. laugh yourselves into _____ (*Twelfth Night*, III, 2, 73)

21. loved not _____ but too well (*Othello*, V, 2, 344)
22. masters of their _____ (*Julius Caesar*, I, 2, 139)
23. melted into _____, into thin _____ (*The Tempest*, IV, 1, 150)
24. milk of human _____ (*Macbeth*, I, 5, 17)
25. more sinned against than _____ (*King Lear*, III, 2, 60)

26. neither rhyme nor _____ (*The Comedy of Errors*, II, 2, 48)
27. I'll not _____ an inch (*The Taming of the Shrew*, I, 11, 14)
28. one fell _____ (*Macbeth*, IV, 3, 219)
29. a pair of star-_____ lovers (*Romeo and Juliet*, Prologue, 6)
30. parting is such sweet _____ (*Romeo and Juliet*, II, 2, 184)

31. a plague on both your _____ (*Romeo and Juliet*, III, 1, 95)
32. pomp and _____ (*Othello*, III, 3, 354)
33. a pound of _____ (*The Merchant of Venice*, IV, 1, 307)
34. the quality of mercy is not _____ (*The Merchant of Venice*, IV, 1, 184)
35. salad _____ (*Antony and Cleopatra*, I, 5, 73)

36. short _____ (*Richard III*, III, 4, 97)
37. a sorry _____ (*Macbeth*, II, 2, 22)
38. spotless _____ (*Richard II*, I, 1, 178)
39. strange _____ (*The Tempest*, II, 2, 40)
40. too much of a good _____ (*As You Like It*, IV, 1, 124)

41. a tower of _____ (*Richard III*, V, 3, 12)
42. uneasy lies the head that wears a _____ (*Henry IV, Part 2*, III, 1, 31)
43. the most unkindest _____ of all (*Julius Caesar*, III, 2, 183)
44. wear my heart upon my _____ (*Othello*, I, 1, 64)
45. what _____ these mortals be (*A Midsummer's Night Dream*, III, 2, 115)

46. what the _____! (*The Merry Wives of Windsor*, III, 2, 15)
47. what's _____ is _____ (*Macbeth*, III, 2, 12)
48. wild-goose _____ (*Romeo and Juliet*, II, 4, 65)
49. with bated _____ (*The Merchant of Venice*, I, 3, 125)
50. the world's mine _____ (*The Merry Wives of Windsor*, II, 2, 3)

Answers

1. stage 2. luck 3. discretion 4. idiot 5. ice
6. last 7. circle 8. smooth 9. home 10. inch
11. goodness 12. conclusion 13. monster 14. days 15. words
16. play on 17. variety 18. palm 19. trowel 20. stitches
21. wisely 22. fates 23. air 24. kindness 25. sinning
26. reason 27. budge 28. swoop 29. crossed 30. sorrow
31. houses 32. circumstance 33. flesh 34. strained 35. days
36. shrift 37. sight 38. reputation 39. bedfellows 40. thing
41. strength 42. crown 43. cut 44. sleeve 45. fools
46. dickens 47. done 48. chase 49. breath 50. oyster

SHAKESPEAREAN RIDDLES

It has been said that a million monkeys at a million keyboards could produce the complete works of William Shakespeare. Today, thanks to the internet, we know that is not true.

Shakespeare was a great riddler. His most famous stumper tricks some of his characters in *The Merchant of Venice*. The father of the young, beautiful, and quick-witted heiress Portia concocts a puzzle to ensure that his daughter marries a worthy suitor. He requires that any suitor for her hand in marriage must choose one of three caskets: One casket is gold, one silver, and one made of lead. In one casket reposes a portrait of Portia, and only the suitor who selects that casket may marry her.

On the gold casket appears this message: "Who chooseth me shall gain what many men desire." On the silver casket: "Who chooseth me shall get as much as he deserves." On the lead casket: "Who chooseth me must give and hazard all he hath."

The lead casket turns out to be the one that holds Portia's picture. Since the riddle said that the chooser of lead "must give and hazard all he hath," Portia's father knows that the man who picks that casket will be willing to make sacrifices and work hard to build a successful marriage. It just so happens that this lucky suitor is Bassanio, the very man Portia herself loves.

How many of these fifteen riddles about the Bard can you solve?

1. What do you call a nervous javelin throw?

2. How do we know that William Shakespeare was a pun master?

3. How do we know that Shakespeare's wife was also quite verbal?

4. How do we know that Shakespeare must have been a very fast writer?

5. How do we know that Shakespeare threw tantrums?

6. What was Shakespeare's phone number?

7. What was Shakespeare's favorite video game?

8. What did the math textbook say to the Shakespeare textbook?

9. What happened when Shakespeare started writing poetry?

10. What did Shakespeare say when someone asked him if he was writing a sonnet in pentameter?

11. When translated into Arabic, what is the meter of Shakespeare's sonnets?

12. The Bard owned a sporting goods store. What was its ad for the January sale?

13. Shakespeare and The Beatles walk into a bar. What does the bartender say?

14. Why did Shakespeare enjoy English class in high school?

15. Why was Shakespeare a good teammate to have?

Answers

1. Shake Spear 2. He created many plays on words. 3. Because Anne Hath A Way with words. 4. He was always making a scene. 5. He died on the same day he was born (April 23, 1564, and April 23, 1616).

6. Fie fie fie, et tu et tu. 7. Sonnet the Hedgehog. 8. "Look, drama king. I've already got enough problems, and I really don't need any of your tragedies." 9. He went from Bard to verse. 10. "Iamb."

11. Islamic pentameter. 12. "Now is the winter of our discount tents." 13. "Sorry, you're barred and those four guys are banned." 14. He didn't have to study Shakespeare. 15. He would always play write.

What happened to the young Shakespearean couple who went out for dinner and found that the guy had forgotten his wallet? It ended up that Romee owed what Julie et.

Here are fifteen more riddles that involve Shakespeare's plays and characters.

1. What is Romeo and Juliet's least favorite fruit?
2. What's the difference between COVID-19 and *Romeo and Juliet*?
3. Why would the witches in Macbeth make terrible baseball umpires?
4. What did Lady Macbeth say to her dog?
5. What's the best cleaning product on the market?

6. Who is the greatest chicken killer in Shakespeare?
7. What's the title of Shakespeare's play about a small pig in a small village?
8. Why did Shakespeare write *Hamlet* with a quill pen rather than a pencil?
9. In *Hamlet*, what are the gravediggers engaging in when they unearth the remains of Yorick?
10. What did Julius Caesar say when Brutus asked him how many doughnuts he had eaten?

11. What did Julius Caesar die of?
12. What did Cleopatra sing when she clasped the asp to her breast?
13. In what Shakespeare play are loyal people embarrassed?
14. Each summer, what do people say when coronavirus lockdowns are lifted?
15. The title of what Shakespeare play describes this chapter if you enjoyed it, and what other title describes this chapter if it wasn't worth your time?

Answers

1. Cantaloupe. 2. One's the coronavirus, and the other's a Verona crisis. 3. Because they think that "Fair is foul and foul is fair." 4. "Out, damned Spot! Out, I say!" 5. Lady Macbeth Spot Remover.

6. Macbeth, because he did murder most fowl. 7. *Hamlet.* 8. Because pencils confused him: 2B or not 2B. 9. Skull duggery. 10. "Et two, Brutus."

11. stabbing pains. 12. "Fangs for the Mammaries!" 13. *The Shaming of the True.* 14. "Once more unto the beach, dear friends!" 15. *As You Like It* and *Much Ado About Nothing.*

NAME THAT TUNE!

William Shakespeare shuffled off his mortal coil more than four centuries ago, yet his characters continue to enthrall and entertain us today. Match each Shakespearean character with the appropriate tune. Banquo's theme song, for example, would be "Ghost in My Head."

1. Ariel   "Can't Buy Me Love"
2. Bottom   "Circle of Life"
3. Caliban   "Come Fly With Me"
4. Calpurnia   "Crazy"
5. Cleopatra   "Everybody Plays the Fool"
6. Falstaff   "Fat Jack"
7. Hamlet   "First Cut is the Deepest"
8. Henry V   "The Hunch"
9. Iago   "I Dreamed a Dream"
10. Jaques   "If I Were a Boy"
11. Julius Caesar   "I'm Just a Country Boy"
12. King Lear   "I Put a Spell on You"
13. Macbeth   "I Will Always Love You"
14. Ophelia "   Jealousy (Look What You Have Done to Me)"
15. Orsino   "Leader of the Pack"
16. Othello   "Liar Liar"
17. Portia   "Mack the Knife"
18. Prospero   "Money, Money, Money"

19. Richard III   "Monster Mash"
20. Romeo and Juliet   "Play That Funky Music"
21. Rosalind   "Send In the Clowns"
22. Shylock   "Think Too Much"
23. The Three Witches   "This Old Man"
24. Touchstone   "Walk Like an Egyptian"
25. Yorick   "We're Off to See the Wizard"

Answers

1. Ariel: "Come Fly with Me" 2. Bottom: "Send In the Clowns" 3. Caliban: "Monster Mash" 4. Calpurnia: "I Dreamed a Dream" 5. Cleopatra: "Walk Like an Egyptian"

6. Falstaff: "Fat Jack" 7. Hamlet: "Think Too Much" 8. Henry V: "Leader of the Pack" 9. Iago: "Liar Liar" 10. Jaques: "Circle of Life"

11. Julius Caesar: "First Cut is the Deepest" 12. King Lear: "This Old Man" 13. Macbeth: "Mack the Knife" 14. Ophelia: "Crazy" 15. Orsino: "Play That Funky Music"

16. Othello: "Jealousy" 17. Portia: "Can't Buy Me Love" 18. Prospero: "We're Off to See the Wizard" 19. Richard III: "The Hunch" 20. Romeo and Juliet: "I Will Always Love You"

21. Rosalind: "If I Were a Boy" 22. Shylock: "Money, Money, Money" 23. The Three Witches: "I Put a Spell On You" 24. Touchstone: "I'm Just a Country Boy" 25. Yorick: "Everybody Plays the Fool"

SHAKESPEARE IN THE NEWS

In the fall of 2017, the Houston Astros baseball team, in its fifty-sixth season, won their first World Series by defeating the Los Angeles Dodgers four games to three.

Three years later it came to light that throughout the 2017 season video-room staffers for the Astros organization used a center-field camera to steal signs from opposing teams' catchers. A story in 2020 led off: "Baseball demanded a pound of flesh from the Houston Astros, who for months showed little remorse for a sign-stealing scandal that rocked the sport and tainted their 2017 World Series win over the Dodgers." The reference to "a pound of flesh" illustrates how robustly William Shakespeare, who died more than four centuries ago, is living in our language.

In Shakespeare's *The Merchant of Venice*, the moneylender Shylock demands that he be paid the pound of flesh promised as collateral for a loan to Antonio. Unfortunately for Shylock, the judge grants the pound of flesh, but only if not a single drop of blood is spilled.

Now identify the plays echoed in each of the news stories below.

1. Donald Trump is not a Caesar. He does not bestride our narrow world like a colossus.

2. In the last four years, we've created six million new jobs!" cries the Great Communicator, and the rabble hiss and clap and throw up their sweaty nightcaps.

3. In a collection of his journalism, "Lend Me Your Ears," British Prime Minister Boris Johnson describes his free-market approach.

4. THE KINDEST CUT OF ALL (headline for an article about laser surgery).

5. RAND PAUL SPARS WITH DR. FAUCI DURING SENATE HEARING: "I don't think you're the end-all'."

6. EUROPE FALLS ONCE MORE INTO THE BREACH (headline for an article about European disunity)

7. If it is sleep that knits up the raveled sleeve of care, then an overwhelming number of Americans are walking around with distinctly tatty shirt cuffs.

8. ALL THE WORLD'S THEIR STAGE (headline for article about international terrorists).

9. It is one of his most endearing personal qualities that Joe Biden wears his emotions on his sleeve.

10. THE GOVERNOR, THE CONVICT, AND THE QUALITY OF MERCY (headline of a story about a governor and a death-row convict).

Answers

The first four allusions are to Shakespeare's tragedy *Julius Caesar.*

1. In I, 2, 143, Cassius laments in: "Why, man, he doth bestride the narrow world/Like a Colossus, and we petty men/Walk under his huge legs and peep about/To find ourselves dishonorable graves."

2. In I, 2, 246, Casca vividly describes to Brutus the crowd's visceral reaction when Caesar refuses the emperor's crown: "And still, as he refused it, the rabblement hooted and clapped their chapped hands and threw up their sweaty night-caps and uttered such a deal of stinking breath because Caesar refused the crown that it had almost choked Caesar—for he swooneded and fell down at it."

The next two allusions pluck elements from Marc Antony's funeral oration:

3. "Friends, Romans, countrymen, lend me your ears!/I come to bury Caesar, not to praise him." (III, 2, 74-75).

4. Marc Antony points to Caesar's pierced body and cries, "This was the most unkindest cut of all." (III, 2, 183).

5. Senator Paul's statement echoes *Macbeth,* I, 7, 5o in which the ambitious Thane of Cawdor soliloquizes about assassinating Duncan so as to become king: "that but this blow [the murder] might be the be-all and the end-all."

6. Henry V exhorts his troops at Harfleur, "Once more unto the breach, dear friends, once more/Or close the wall up with our English dead." (*Henry V,* III, 1, 1).

7. Macbeth laments his loss of "sleep that knits up the ravel'd sleeve of care." (*Macbeth,* II, 2, 34).

8. Jacques muses on life in a dramatic fashion: "All the world's a stage,/And all the men and women merely players." (*As You Like It,* II, 7, 138).

9. The arch villain Iago pretends that he is just a naive man who "will wear my heart upon my sleeve." (*Othello,* I, 1, 56).

10. Disguised as a judge, Portia proclaims, "The quality of mercy is not strain'd./It droppeth as the gentle rain from heaven." (*The Merchant of Venice,* IV, 1, 184).

CLASSIC LITERARY LOVERS

DYNAMIC DUOS

"The war between the sexes is the only one in which both sides regularly sleep with the enemy," observed Quentin Crisp. "Women marry men hoping they will change. Men marry women hoping they will not. So each is inevitably disappointed," concluded Albert Einstein. "Love is a fire. But whether it is going to warm your hearth or burn down your house, you can never tell," quipped Joan Crawford. Whatever your opinion about love, literature swirls with it, and we often draw our images of love from the books we read, most deeply from the ancient books. Here's a final game that brings together the worlds of the Bible, Greek mythology, and William Shakespeare. As a kind of review of the literary span of the last three clusters in this book, try your hand and mind at this quiz about the couples who couple in classic stories.

Starting with Adam and Eve, the Bible has chronicled many a couple. Match the biblical husbands on the left with their biblical wives or lovers on the right. One of these men and one of these women had two spouses.

1. Aaron	Bathsheba
2. Abraham	Delilah
3. Ahasuerus	Dinah
4. Ananias	Elisheba
5. Boaz	Esther
6. David	Gomer
7. Hosea	Leah
8. Isaac	Mary
9. Jacob	Rachel

10. Joakim	Rebecca
11. Joseph	Ruth
12. Moses	Sapphira
13. Samson	Sarah
14. Shechem	Susanna
15. Uriah	Zipporah

Answers

1. Aaron/Elisheba 2. Abraham/Sarah 3. Ahasuerus/Esther 4. Ananias/Sapphira 5. Boaz/Ruth

6. David/Bathsheba 7. Hosea/Gomer 8. Isaac/Rebecca 9. Jacob/Leah and Rachel 10. Joakim/Susanna

11. Joseph/Mary 12. Moses/Zipporah 13. Samson/Delilah 14. Shechem/Dinah 15. Uriah/Bathsheba

Now let's enlist a list of classical couples. Match each mythological man with a mythological woman.

1. Aeneas	Aphrodite
2. Agamemnon	Clytemnestra
3. Deucalion	Deianeira
4. Hades	Dido
5. Hephaestus	Eurydice
6. Hercules	Galatea
7. Leander	Hecuba
8. Odysseus	Helen
9. Oedipus	Hera
10. Orpheus	Hero
11. Paris	Jocasta
12. Priam	Penelope
13. Pygmalion	Persephone
14. Pyramus	Pyrrha
15. Zeus	Thisbe

Answers

1. Aeneas/Dido 2. Agamemnon/Clytemnestra 3. Deucalion/Pyrrha, 4. Hades/Persephone 5. Hephaestus/Aphrodite

6. Hercules/Deianeira 7. Leander/Hero 8. Odysseus/Penelope 9. Oedipus/Jocasta 10. Orpheus/Eurydice

11. Paris/Helen 12. Priam/Hecuba 13. Pygmalion/Galatea 14. Pyramus/Thisbe 15. Zeus/Hera

Now join together these husbands and wives and lovers who people the plays of William Shakespeare.

1. Antony	Audrey
2. Benedick	Beatrice
3. Brutus	Cleopatra
4. Ferdinand	Desdemona
5. Florizel	Hermia
6. Hamlet	Hermione
7. Henry V	Katharina
8. Leontes	Katharine
9. Lysander	Miranda
10. Oberon	Ophelia
11. Orlando	Perdita
12. Orsino	Portia
13. Othello	Rosalind
14. Petruchio	Titania
15. Touchstone	Viola

Answers

1. Antony/Cleopatra 2. Benedick/Beatrice 3. Brutus/Portia 4. Ferdinand/Miranda 5. Florizel/Perdita

6. Hamlet/Ophelia 7. Henry V/Katharine 8. Leontes/Hermione 9. Lysander/Hermia 10. Oberon/Titania

11. Orlando/Rosalind 12. Orsino/Viola 13. Othello/Desdemona 14. Petruchio/Katharina 15. Touchstone/Audrey

Acknowledgments

I am grateful for permission to adapt in *Richard Lederer's Ultimate Book of Literary Trivia* versions of some items that have appeared in my Viking, Gibbs Smith, and Marion Street Press books. Thousands of thanks to Caroline McCullagh, Megan Edwards, Charles Patton, and Eileen Breedlove for their loving labors to make my book the very best it could be.

Art credits: cover by Todd Smith; back-cover photograph by Bob Hoffman; Sherlock Holmes and Dr. Watson, by Sidney Paget 1892; daguerreotype of Emily Dickinson, c. early 1847; Rodin's The Thinker in the Sky, by CrisNYCa; The Livraria Lello bookstore; Moses Showing the Ten Commandments, by Gustave Doré 1865; Statue of Zeus by Maarten van Heemskerck 1572; William Shakespeare, by Martin Droeshout 1623; Romeo and Juliet by Ford Madox Brown 1870

AUTHOR BIOGRAPHY

Richard Lederer is the author of more than fifty books about language, history, and humor, including his best-selling *Anguished English* series and his current books, *A Treasury of Halloween Humor,* *A Treasury of Christmas Humor,* *A Pleasury of Word & Phrase Origins,* and *So That's What It Means!* He is a founding co-host of "A Way With Words," broadcast on Public Radio.

Dr. Lederer's syndicated column, "Lederer on Language," appears in newspapers and magazines throughout the United States. He has been named International Punster of the Year and Toastmasters International's Golden Gavel winner.

He lives in San Diego with his wife, Simone van Egeren.

richardhlederer@gmail.com
verbivore.com

www.ingramcontent.com/pod-product-compliance
Lightning Source LLC
Chambersburg PA
CBHW021050090426
42738CB00006B/270